SWAPPING HOUSEWIVES

S W A P P I N G
H O U S E W I V E S

Rachel and Jacob and Leah

V a s h t i   M u r p h y   M c K e n z i e

THE PILGRIM PRESS
CLEVELAND

Dedication

—◆—

To Stan McKenzie,

My beloved husband: best prayer partner,
best friend, best listener, and best foot massager
in the whole world!

To all married couples
who are covenanted and committed
to a sacred shared adventure
with Jesus Christ.

The Pilgrim Press, 700 Prospect Avenue, Cleveland, Ohio 44115-1100
thepilgrimpress.com
© 2007 by Vashti Murphy McKenzie

All names in this book have been changed to protect the identities
of the individuals.

♻ Printed in the United States of America on acid-free paper that contains
post-consumer fiber.

11   10   09   08   07   5   4   3   2   1

Library of Congress Cataloging-in-Publication Data

McKenzie, Vashti M., 1947–
    Swapping housewives : Rachel and Jacob and Leah / Vashti Murphy McKenzie.
        p. cm.
        ISBN-13: 978-0-8298-1773-7 (alk. paper)
        1. Bible. O.T. Genesis XXIX–XXX—Criticism, interpretation, etc.   2. Family
—Biblical teaching.   3. Rachel (Biblical matriarch)   4. Jacob (Biblical patriarch)
5. Leah (Biblical matriarch)   6. Marriage—Biblical teaching.   I. Title.
BS1238.F34M35 2007
222'.1106—dc22   2007015944

CONTENTS

PREFACE

The ancient marriage mayhem of Jacob to Rachel and Leah and later to their servants, Bilhah and Zilpah, is explored and paralleled with 21st century relationships. In today's American culture, the institution of marriage is on life support. Statistically, there are just as many couples who are cohabitating as there are couples who are getting married.

To many people, marriage is a sacred covenant commitment that becomes a shared adventure with Jesus Christ. Millions of couples are navigating their relationships from the shark infested waters of marital bliss to calm waters and balmy temperatures. They have survived the rough seas of trials and temptations and have emerged stronger spiritually and emotionally.

And yes, there are those who crash and burn after takeoff.

To some, marriage has been reduced to a contract with limited term options. Living together is equated as "trial marriages," and "starter wives"—the current terms that have entered into the cultural vernacular.

In my various roles over the past thirty years, I have heard the testimonies and triumphs of countless men and women who are in covenant relationships. I have heard them as a workshop leader, seminar instructor, preacher, pastor, married couples and women's ministry facilitator, and now as Bishop.

I have also seen the tears of couples who have wrestled with complex marital, moral, and spiritual issues. They have wrestled with themselves, cultural expectations, and spouses and children in a community that shouts: "We belong together but maybe not forever." "We belong together—sometimes." "We belong together but I also like to belong to someone else." "We belong together and I want to continue to sample and share on the other side of the fence and even in another gender."

My husband of thirty-nine years graciously allowed me to share insights from our marriage in exchange for my consenting to a "sho'nuf" two week vacation in Hawaii without a cell phone.

"Wow! He *really* had to twist your arm on that one!" said Agatha Willamette Robinson, fondly called Aunt Agony.

Everyone has a character in their lives and Aunt Agony is mine. Aunt Agony weighs in with her wit and sometimes wisdom in the chapters ahead. She is an unordained, unofficial expert on everything human.

By the Grace of God, I hope you are able to grow and learn as I have in writing this book.

ACKNOWLEDGMENTS

*For I wrote to you out of great distress
and anguish of heart and with many tears,
not to grieve you but to let you know
the depth of my love for you.*

2 Corinthians 2:4

*. . . Writing is exploration; most of the time
I'm surprised where the journey takes me.*

Jack Dann

To be a successful writer, William Faulkner concluded, a writer needs only three things: experience, observation and imagination. Two of the former can supply the lack of any one of the three. Writers also need food, water, sleep and a neck and shoulder massage at regular intervals!

A writer needs vision, the language of the Holy Spirit, support of family, friends and executive staff. I am blessed with a cadre of family, friends and an excellent "home team" in the 13th Episcopal District of the African Methodist Episcopal Church and across the several continents.

Expressions of gratitude are extended to the men and women through various churches and ministries who shared their lives with us. Thanks to the many Circles of Love that have been started to create a special time of "woman sharing." Your cards, letters and e-mails about your book clubs and study groups have been encouraging. It was great to meet so many women on a journey around the world. You can share your thoughts with Aunt Agony at www.auntagony@bellsouth.net.

Thank you to the many covenant couples whose lives have touched both mine and Stan's. We have observed your love and commitment through the years and we praise God for your witness.

Thank you to Rev. Tyronda Burgess, my executive aide, who assisted with some of the aspects of researching and detail tending. Thank you to good friends who helped keep my feet to the fire: Rev. Leah White, Rev. Angelique Mason and to the other Women of the Covenant who continue to sow seeds of inspiration into my life.

Our daughters Rev. Vashti-Jasmine McKenzie and Ms. Joi-Marie McKenzie are emerging creative writers in their own right. Thank you for listening and sharing. Rev. Jazz, thanks for being an exegetical sounding board, and Joi, for your poetry.

To Rev. Katurah Cooper, spiritual daughter and friend, pastor of Empowerment Temple in Monrovia, Liberia, thank you for my Liberian experience. It was a tremendous blessing to see how God functions in political dysfunction. She introduced me to a group of ordinary women who exercised extraordinary courage during the unordinary times of civil strife in Liberia.

Once again, Kim Martin Sadler, the Editorial Director at The Pilgrim Press, is the turnaround queen in publishing. Thank you for who you are and how you allow God to use the extraordinary gifts given to you. Thanks to Janice Brown, director of production, and Robyn Nordstrom for your cover design.

May God continue to bless those who shared their anecdotes and information to complete this project as well as the congregations who heard the initial sermons. Thank you to those who helped in any way, whose names escape me in this hour.

My husband Stan McKenzie is a rare jewel among men. Thank you for your patience while I was under deadline pressure. Thank you for being there at the genesis of this project and for being there for me when I unchained myself from the computer.

I consider this a work in progress. May the Lord speak to your heart and nourish your soul and your relationships.

INTRODUCTION

. . . Bring happiness to the wife he married.

Deuteronomy 24:5

Grow old with me. The best is yet to be. . . .

Robert Browning

My husband Stan and I have been married for thirty-nine years. This is longer than some folk have lived! Stan, a former NBA basketball star, is my best friend, confidant, and playmate. Moreover, Stan is the consoler who is the stabilizing rock to my butterfly ways. And he is also the father of our three grown children.

The pressures of careers and church; community and culture; children and change, can add stress and strain to any relationship. If we had tossed out our marriage at the first thunderstorm, we would have added to the sad and growing statistics on divorce.

Instead of another convenient coupling, our love included a covenant commitment. Covenant relationships are relationships in which love and commitment are two vital ingredients. More importantly, however, the commitment to each other is sustained with God supplying the glue.

Do we support each other's interests? Yes. Do we make sacrifices for each other? Yes. Do we make room for the other's gifts and talents? Yes. Do we know our weaknesses and strengths? Yes. Do we go to bat for each other? Yes. Do we face trouble together? Yes. Do we disagree? Yes. Do we argue? Yes. Do we kiss and make up? Yes.

Do we have a perfect marriage? No. Do we have a very good marriage? Yes. Do we still love each other? Yes, immeasurably!

In the process of pursuing relational happiness, however, sometimes the results are catastrophic.

The challenging, changing and complex world of the 21st century can have a profound impact upon our relationships. This virtual tidal wave of unprecedented change is pounding the shores of what use to be "until death do us part" that resided on the beach of "starter marriages." All of this destruction is taking place at a time when swift transition moves on in an unpredictable course.

So profoundly revolutionary is this new civilization that it challenges all of our old assumptions, our old ways of thinking, and our old formulas. It also challenges our dogmas and ideologies without consideration to how cherished or how useful they were in the past. According to writer and futurist Alvin Toffler, they no longer fit well into the scheme of things. Might this include your marriage?

It is difficult to predict what is going to happen until it happens. Today, couples must mobilize every ounce of intelligence just to stay on top of the cultural matrix. The learning curve is short. If you don't get it, it's gone. You could be left in the dust wondering what happened to your marriage when "for better or worse" got worse before it got better.

Forever is lost in our impatient society. We hope to find that one true love and expect everything to be perfect even with our own imperfections. We compare our relationships and marriages with those we see on television and in movies. We long for intimate bliss, warm fuzzy feelings, talk during dinner about our busy day, deep life changing conversations with our children, and family activities, as well as problems solved in 30 to 60 minute increments. More than likely, what we see on screen may not be what we are getting in real life. Divorce statistics reveal that approximately one out of two marriages end in divorce.

The state of our marriage unions has changed dramatically since 1960. According to the National Marriage Project, the number of African American men married in 1960 was 60.9 percent, and women, 59.8 percent. In 2000, the rate dropped to 42.8 percent married men and to 36.2 percent married women. The overall percentage for all other groups was somewhat above 50 percent. The average age of those who marry has also changed. Young adults are marrying later. The average age of first marriages has risen to 25 years of age for women and 27 years of age for men.

According to the U. S. Census Bureau, in 2002 there were 8.8 million African American families, of which 48 percent were married couple families, and 43 percent were families maintained by women with no spouse present. There are some demographers who predict that 85 percent of all current young adults will marry.

Relationships, including the married kind, have had a rough time. Myths such as the following abound: to maintain long-term marital relationships you need good luck and romantic love; cohabitation is better than "a piece of paper"; children can bring a couple together; singles have more satisfying sexual relationships than married couples; women are more at risk of domestic violence in a marriage than out of a marriage.

The saga of struggling relationships is as old as Adam and Eve. The story of Jacob, Rachael and Leah is an ancient story of struggle and survival. It includes timeless truths about God and humanity.

Swapping Housewives is an excellent book to use in Bible Study, men and women's fellowship meetings or in marriage ministries. It will spark lively discussions in book club sessions or with parents and their young adult children.

Swapping Housewives will also introduce Agatha Willamette Robinson, a woman who has been a friend of mine for many years. She enjoys the moniker of "Aunt Agony." I first met Aunt Agony when our three children were stretched between three separate schools, elementary, middle and high school. After the morning rush of combing hair, making lunch, pressing uniforms and the "Oh, Mom, I forgot that today I'm suppose to brings . . . ," Aunt Agony and I became sisterfriends!

I would look forward to sitting in my mother's kitchen and downloading over a hot cup of tea. It was a 30 minute oasis prior to going to my office where I would have to face another morning rush of daily problems—all waiting to be solved by me and God.

When my mother suddenly died, I missed our morning time together. It was a blessed moment to dialog with someone who had always known me and who loved me just the same. She was a great listener and I was a good talker.

As the 9:00 A.M. time approached and the work of the day called to me, mother would lay her best advice on the table. It was not sugarcoated sweetheart stuff. Her words of wisdom cut through all of my defenses and veiled concerns. And as always, it went straight to the heart of the matter.

My daily pit stop and pick-me-up was gone. Believe it or not, we preachers need someone to preach to us too! Nevertheless, I still needed liquid caffeine to jumpstart my day. I first found it at those quick stop places where all the snacks that can expand your waistline live. Then I found a little café on a corner near where I lived.

It was a nondescript place on my regular route to work, with antiques in the window that changed with the seasons. I first thought that the owners were school teachers because the café was always decorated for the appropriate occasion. There were cut out hearts in February, shamrocks in March, colored eggs and baskets in April . . . you get the picture. I soon found out that it wasn't the owner who had an eye for interior decorating. It was Agatha Willamette Robinson who proudly explained to me that she got her middle name from a river in Oregon.

Every morning, the tables that looked handmade were adorned with fresh clean table linen. The stools at the short counter were very retro looking—you know, that 1950ish look. Agatha was the reining queen. She was the head waitress who seemed to know every customer on a first name basis.

Like all the morning commuters, I would slip in and stand at the edge of the counter to place my usual order—"A large tea, Earl Grey, if you have it, crème and sugar, heavy on the crème."

One morning, the smell of eggs, scrapple (it's a Baltimore breakfast meat) and grits grabbed me by the collar and threw me down at a corner table where the sun warmed my face. Agatha came over and muttered a comment about "it's about time you ate some food as skinny as you are." I was skinny then but not now. If you knew me, you would know that this encounter took place a long time ago.

We became friends during the ten years I served as pastor of Payne Memorial AME Church. Agatha served tea, breakfast, and her spin on what was happening in the world. She peppered her comments with words like "sweetie" and "hun"—which is another Baltimore thing. Agatha gave new meaning to spandex and leopard prints—the style of clothing that she wore over her own skinny frame. Her apron was always starched beyond reason. Her hair was severely pulled back from her face into a bun and a number two pencil stuck out of its side.

Agatha was born and raised in Baltimore. After graduating from Patterson Park High School, she began her hospitality career. She matured in the University of Hard Knocks and learned about life in the streets.

Agatha admitted to being fifty but she was closer to eighty years of age. She had outlived three husbands and was afraid to marry her boyfriend because in Agatha's words, "I want him to live a little longer."

She earned her nickname Aunt Agony because everyone who came into the little café on the corner trusted her with their "agonies." She would listen patiently while serving biscuits and gravy, bagels and cream cheese or creamed chipped beef—another Baltimore thing. When she handed you the check, she also handed you her opinion about your agony.

Aunt Agony has heard it all. She had heard stories about jealous spouses, conniving co-workers, obsessed boyfriends, financial disappointments, rape and incest.

One morning, a father and daughter, who were occasional customers, took a seat in the café. The father ordered breakfast for both and went to use the men's room. The little girl, who looked about 12, passed a note to Aunt Agony that simply said, "He rapes me." By the time the father came out of the restroom there were police officers waiting for him. Aunt Agony made the call.

Aunt Agony makes her debut in *Swapping Housewives* because she provides an excellent balance between the sacred and the secular. Aunt Agony answers at least one question in her own inimitable style.

There are a series of questions at the end of each chapter which can be used for individual or group study.

Each chapter also concludes with *S.M.A.R.T Moves.* S.M.A.R.T stands for "Spiritual Motivation and Action for Real Transformation." This section is intended as a tool to keep God at the center of your relationships. *Talking Points* will allow you to engage in conversation about the issues discussed in each chapter. *The Word of Prayer* and *The Word of God* can be used to uplift your spiritual experience.

Let me share why S.M.A.R.T Moves is so important to me. I am the kind of person who once awake is fully awake. It doesn't matter whether it is 3:00 A.M. or 8:00 A.M., when the grace of God returns consciousness to my mind, it rapidly kicks into gear. While sleeping, it seems like my unconscious mind has been placed on pause. My mind can rewind and replay all my challenges and worries about the next problem on the horizon.

The late Bishop Harrison Bryant took a daily nap. Many years ago, he passed the suggestion along to me. It was just a power pause—a pause to push away the world; offering time to relax the mind and body. I have tried it. God knows I have tried the "mid-day nap strategy." Regretfully, it takes too long for me to get to sleep and it is not long enough for me to rest. It has worked for Bishop Bryant and others, but not for me.

What works for me are small daily moments. I call them S.M.A.R.T Moves. Howard Thurman calls such a moment "centering down." He writes that it is good to center down and sit quietly to see one's self pass by. It is a pause in the day that I take to realign myself with God's will.

I take S.M.A.R.T Moves in the office, on airplanes, in waiting rooms and lulls in meetings. It is an easy way to refresh my thinking and recharge my battery. In private, I like to put on my favorite inspirational or gospel music. In public, I can hear the music as it moves my heart. Often, I find by the end of the day, I am not weighed down by crises or challenges. I have a new scripture memory verse or song living in my heart.

Taking S.M.A.R.T Moves is a thanksgiving, praise and prayer break. It is a few minutes of thanksgiving to lift your level of gratitude for God's unfailing love, a pause to praise God for who God is, what God has done, and what God can do. It is a minute prayer to keep lines of communication open with heaven for any further instructions, marching orders, or recalibration of attitude and activities.

In my book *Journey to the Well,* I advocated taking a daily Sabbath. The discipline to take a daily Sabbath could take between 30 minutes to more than an hour. Doing S.M.A.R.T Moves takes three to five minutes. The study questions can be done separate from the prayer, praise and thanksgiving. Take as much time as you want on the questions whether or not they are done alone or with someone else.

S.M.A.R.T continues with Aunt Agony's advice. In her own style of wit and humor, she suggests daily steps to enhance relationships with *Foreplay, Pillow Talk, Kiss and Tell, Kiss and Make Up, Marital Madness,* and *Singularity.*

Foreplay includes an activity to start the day. *Pillow Talk* is something that can be done in the evening alone, with a friend or spouse. *Kiss and Tell* will either be self-disclosure activities or positive affirmations for you to use alone or with someone else. *Kiss and Make Up* is just what the name suggests. It discusses how to reconcile when things do not go according to plan. *Marital Madness* discusses the things couples do to drive each other crazy in their relationship. Lastly, *Singularity* is Aunt Agony's hints and tips for unattached individuals.

God took a stroll in the Garden of Eden. Mark says that Jesus went apart from his Disciples to pray. John records that Jesus sat down in the heat of the day at Jacob's well. With the cross on the horizon, the Messiah prayed in the Garden of Gethsemane. Today, the Psalmist advises us to: "Be still. . . ."

Aunt Agony says, "Hun, if you don't stop long enough to rotate your tires, you'll end up flat." May you learn from Rachel, Jacob, and Leah and develop stronger, spirit-led relationships.

ONE

GOD HAS THE LAST WORD

Now, my son, listen carefully and do what I tell you.

Genesis 26:9

(Read Genesis 29 and 30)

People are what their mothers make them.

Ralph Waldo Emerson

The story of Jacob, Rachel, and Leah begins with actions that manipulated the future of a family and subsequently a nation. Much in the same way Ray manipulated the life of this wife.

When Annette married Ray, she was active in the church. She was a member of our women's ministry Circle of Love. Annette sang in the choir and taught Church School. She had frequently come to our "Call to the Wall," the 6:00 A.M. prayer service, and our annual "Lock In" of prayer, praise, preaching and teaching.

Gradually Annette pulled away from one ministry after another. Her work schedule or her home responsibilities were her excuses. She left the choir. She stopped going to lunch with her friends. She even limited her frequent visits to her parents to once a year.

It was Annette's sudden weight loss that made everyone concerned. She wouldn't talk about what was happening in her life. No one suspected that her new husband was systematically cutting her off from the outside world.

A year later I got the call that Annette had tried to commit suicide. It was then that Ray's extreme controlling nature was revealed. Ray was methodical and diabolical. He took her pay checks and put her on an allowance because she wasn't smart enough to handle money. He picked out her clothes and chose her makeup and hairstyle because she had no sense of style. He made plans to host a dinner party at their home with his friends without telling her. When his friends arrived, he told Annette that she forgot, just like the other important things that she always forgot. Ray would tell his friends that this was another symptom to prove that Annette was losing her mind.

Ray controlled Annette by convincing her that people were talking about her behind her back. He told her that her friends were jealous of their marriage and really did not like her. And he convinced her that she did not have time for anyone or anything else because their house had to be cleaned a certain way—Ray's way.

Ray was never physically abusive. It was Ray's emotional abuse that was killing Annette. In Ray's eyes, Annette could do nothing right. Annette thought about getting help but she was too embarrassed to talk to anyone about her situation.

There are people who are devotees of control. These people have a desperate need to hold onto order; any order—irrespective of how it will help or harm someone. Ray had Annette in a controlled environment, albeit negative, but it became the only order she knew.

In this chapter, the issue of control and manipulative behavior will be explored. These two critical issues were at the genesis of events that precipitated Jacob's need to swap housewives. This chapter will also look at living beyond the negative behavior patterns that you might have experienced in your childhood and family. It will end with Aunt Agony's words of wisdom on how to resolve present pains without placing blame on the past.

Oftentimes, things happen to us that are beyond our control. We don't like to think this way or believe it, but it is true. Our human nature would make us think that we are the captains of our fate and the rulers of our destiny.

We like to control our environment, our friends and family members, our neighbors and neighborhoods. This is not new. As infants, we quickly learned how to control our environment. If we cried, someone would come to care for us. By the age of two, we could control a shopping trip with a temper tantrum. And we could upset the entire household with one little word, "No." We lived by the Burger King philosophy: "We can have it our way."

If God would let us, we would try to control the sunrise and the sunset, the rising of the moon, and the twinkle of the stars. If we could, we would control the ebb and flow of the tides, the shade of blue of a cloudless sky, the repertoire of the angel's songs, and the tilt of the halo of the saints; and even God's actions!

Truthfully, some things are beyond our control. As a whole, we cling to the belief that there ought to be some fundamental order in the universe and certainly under our direct control, and there ought to be order in our own life. At the very center of this orderly process is deliberateness and predictability. And along with predictability comes responsibility.

We find comfort in order because the absence of order is chaos. If chaos ruled, our life would be a series of accidents or coincidences that could lead towards recklessness. Such recklessness is an escape plan from responsibility towards nature, God, and ourselves.

When things are beyond our control, it becomes forced chaos. Forced chaos unnerves us; makes us feel vulnerable, helpless; and takes us out of our orderly comfort zones. This may be one of the reasons why we become such devotees of control.

Do you know someone who is a control freak? Did you go to school with control freaks? Do you work with control freaks? Do you live with control freaks? Are you a control freak?

We do crazy things when we feel helplessly out of control or vulnerable. We either hold on too tight or let it all hang out. We become confused about direction and destination. We stay too long or leave too soon, go when we are wanted or stay when we are not wanted. We do not like feeling out of control.

We fail to recognize the number of things that are beyond our control. In many cases, the beginning of life and the end of it are beyond our control; the color of our eyes and hair are beyond our control; our height and body types are beyond our control

Our parents and the number of siblings, or the lack thereof, is beyond our control. So is where a tornado touches down or the path of a hurricane; where lightning will strike or the number of sunny days in a calendar year; the temperature of the ocean; the number of grains of sand on the beach; the number of fish in the seas; the number of times your heart beats in a lifetime; the syncopated rhythm of your breathing; the future of a child; the manner of death of your parents; and the life span of an idea whose time has come are all beyond our control.

No one controls hurricanes like Katrina and Rita, and no one could control water rushing from a broken levee.

Pharaoh tried to keep God's people in bondage in Goshen. Joseph's brothers tried to control the result of his dream by killing the dreamer and the dream. The disciples tried to keep the children off the Messiah's lap but it was beyond their control. And they tried to control a blind man sitting beside the road. They told him to stop calling the name of Jesus. They also tried to keep as Syrophoenician woman from pestering Jesus about her daughter, but it too was beyond their control.

The Pharisees tried to control the rise of a young prophet by the name of Jesus, but it was beyond their control. They also tried to stop the people from waving palms and praising Jesus as he entered Jerusalem. Judas tried to control Jesus by forcing a revolution.

The Sanhedrin court thought they could control the Ruler of rulers and the Lord of Lords. They thought they had him on the cross and in the tomb. The devil thought he had him in hell, but there are some things beyond control. Early that fateful Sunday morning, Jesus rose with all power in his hands! No one controls the resurrection!

The issue of things beyond our control rises to the surface in the book of Genesis, chapters 26–30. Genesis records two types of events. There are events with cosmic ramifications, such as the flood or the destruction of Sodom and Gomorrah. The second are events that are of a personal nature, such as Cain killing his brother Able or Abraham's vision. The first is global and the second is isolated within a country or region. The latter can often be reduced to family matters.

The story of Jacob and Esau begins in struggle. The story implies that the two boys tried to control their order of birth while in the womb. Esau won the struggle in utero. When the patriarch of the family begins to prepare for his death, Abraham's wife Rebekah tries to control the conferring of rights, privileges and family leadership through deceptive means.

Rebekah is a controller. She believes she is justified because of a previous oracle given by God in Genesis, Chapter 25.

Controlling personalities often are those who refuse to be vulnerable. They are afraid of chaos so they arrange other people's lives to their advantage and for their benefit. Like Ray, they make decisions for others or become abusively domineering like Martin Burney. Martin was a wealthy businessman (played chillingly by actor Patrick Bergen) who was extremely abusive and controlling of his wife Laura (Julia Roberts) in the movie *Sleeping with the Enemy*.

Aptly named the trickster, Jacob had a way of controlling events by manipulating life to his advantage. At the behest of his mother, Rebekeh, he plotted for the birthright and the blessing from his father.

Jacob's brother Esau, however, may have helped the situation. His marriages, without parental consent to two Hittite women, could have nudged his mother to favor Jacob. Esau traded what could only be obtained by birth for a bowl of soup. Esau's hunger blinded him. So for a bowl of soup, he gave away what was precious and permanent, his first born status, for something that was transitory—hunger!.

Esau's stomach determined what he valued the most. Satisfying his appetite took precedent over fulfilling his birthright. His hunger controlled his priorities. He reached for what was temporal rather than what was permanent with enduring qualities.

Oftentimes, we make grave mistakes when we allow our appetite to overrule our common sense. Our hunger for money, sex, and power can erode our relationships with God and others. Commitments become like Teflon. We fail to stick with people because our urges allow what is truly important to slide away.

It is possible that our worldly minds want what doesn't belong to us; we reach for what is not ours or give away what is not ours to give.

Chantel gave away her family's heirlooms. Antique jewelry, silver tea services, and fine china were kept behind locked doors in her family's home. They had been handed down in her family for generations.

Chantel did not see the value of keeping them locked away when she could pawn them for easy cash. She was caught up in a lifestyle that demanded ready cash. It had nothing to do with an addiction to drugs, alcohol or gambling. She ran around with friends in a higher income bracket than her family.

As a college student, she had to have a new outfit or bauble to show off. Now in her early thirties, she continues to live in a credit card economy rather than a cash economy. On her visits home to see her elderly father, she always leaves with an antique ring, earrings, watches, fine china or a piece of silver. Of course, she has great intentions of buying it all back—one day—and she will secretly put it all back in the locked cabinets, drawers, and safes. But, of course, the "one day" never arrived.

When Chantel's father died, his will indicated that he had known about Chantel's dirty little secret. He felt she had already received her inheritance and left her nothing. The property and other heirlooms were given to her younger siblings. Instead of being the executor of the estate, she lost that privilege when she started to pilfer the family's inheritance. In reality, she only took what her father allowed her to take. The more valuable items had been removed to safer places soon after the initial items were taken ten years earlier when she was in college.

Chantel's life is somewhat similar to that of the prodigal son. She never came to herself. No, Chantel didn't have the slop hogs experience of the younger son who asked for his inheritance in advance of his father's death. She ended up declaring bankruptcy. Her money-minded friends cut her loose immediately when the money was gone. This should have been a serious wake up call.

One day, Chantel sobbed out the whole story in my office. She, however, could not see how she had cheated herself and her family. In her world, it was okay. Her appetite for things overruled her sense of what was right and what was wrong.

In Jacob's world, it was okay for him to cheat. He obtained his brothers birthright and his father's blessing by using deceptive means. Like Chantel, Jacob took advantage of his father's age. Jacob took advantage of his father's impaired vision to trick him into the blessing ritual.

In the Hebrew Bible, the word for "blessing" appears 600 times. In the context of government, the ruler blessed the ruled. In the context of religion, the priests enacted the privilege to bestow the blessing upon the worshipper. In family matters, it was the father who blessed his wife and children.

The blessing ritual began with food. It ended with the bestowing of the blessing, a sign of special favor that gave direction to the destiny of the recipient.

In the book of Genesis, the writer uses a series of terms to create a story filled with a vocabulary that paints a picture through touching and hearing. "Come near so I can touch you, my son, to know whether you are really my son Esau or not." (Genesis 27:21) "The voice is the voice of Jacob, but the hands are the hands of Esau." (Genesis 27:22)

The writer continues with tasting and smelling. Isaac asked the son he believed to be Esau to come to him for a kiss. When he caught the smell of his clothes, he blessed him, "Ah the smell of my son. . . ." (Genesis 27:27)

Jacob presented his father with the requested meal of game. He also involved Yahweh in the ruse. He falsely claimed that his father's God gave him success in obtaining the meal of game so quickly. "The Lord your God gave me success." (Genesis 27:20)

Exit Jacob and enter Esau with a meal and the expectation of the blessing. When Esau finds out that that both he and his father had been tricked, Esau demands a blessing as well but not a retraction. It is perhaps believed that once given, the blessing is like a bullet shot from an automatic weapon. It cannot be retrieved before it has hit its mark.

Esau's decided to sooth his soul by killing Jacob when his father died. Killing controls the result of the promise. Kill Jacob and kill the promise.

This is an interesting solution that is later carried over into Jacob's family. Jacob would later become the father of twelve. He would favor Rachel's son, Joseph, over all of Leah's sons.

Leah's sons become jealous of the father's attention to Joseph and the dream God gave him that essentially usurps their birthright. It leads them to a similar diabolical plot. The Joseph problem can be solved by killing the dreamer and the dream. Instead, they sell the young Joseph to a passing caravan. They then set up their own ruse to convince their father that Joseph had died.

Again, this behavior is perpetuated in the lives of Saul, who is from Rachel's lineage and David, Leah's descendent. Saul, Israel's first ruler, sought to kill David, who had been secretly anointed by the prophet Samuel to be Israel's second ruler. This pattern of conflict continues within the family unit when David's son Absalom plotted and temporarily gained his father's throne. Some family dysfunctions can repeat themselves even to future generations.

Jacob's manipulative ways successfully led him around his brother and father. Rebekah learned that Esau desired to kill his brother. She believed that Esau will make good on his threat.

Clearly, the family could not effectively communicate with each other. Rebekah spoke to Jacob rather than Esau about the future. She doesn't speak to Isaac, who is portrayed as a humble personality testing his son's identity before giving his blessing. A few scholars surmise that at this point, Issac is a powerless patriarchal figure easily fooled in his latter days.

It isn't until after Jacob's life is threatened by his brother that Rebekah speaks to her husband. Isaac spoke to his sons individually but not together. Word of the threat on Jacob's life comes indirectly, not directly. There may have been messages passed among servants or other family members. It is also quite possible that Rebekah listened at the threshold of the family tents.

Jacob's mother intercedes once again. She directed him to flee to her ancestral home in Haran until the wounds of her oldest son healed. Rebekah realized that she could lose both sons to an untimely death. If Esau killed his brother after Isaac died then Esau would be executed. Her hope was that Esau's temper would cool soon enough for her to see Jacob again. This never happened. Rebekah would never see Jacob again.

Rebekah finally spoke to her husband. She talked to him about her concerns for Jacob's future and not about the threat to his life. She indicated that Esau's two marriages had made her life bitter. She feared that Jacob may do the same.

Isaac spoke to Jacob. He enjoined him from marrying outside of their familial community. He entreated him to go to Haran to marry a cousin, the daughter of his mother's uncle, Laban. This gave legitimacy for Jacob's hasty departure.

Isaac blessed his son for the journey. The father elaborated on the blessing using the language of the covenant God gave him. It is a blessing without reproach for the former deception.

Esau learns that Jacob had obeyed both parents. He took a third wife from the family of Ishmael, seeking to return to the family's good graces.

Jacob left home with his parent's blessing and his brother's hatred. Along the way God transformed an ordinary stone and an ordinary place as Jacob stops on his journey from Beersheba to Haran. Jacob dreams of a stairway with ascending and descending divine beings. Yahweh speaks to Jacob referring to his family, Abraham being the father, not Isaac. Jacob has the same relationship to Abraham as Isaac. The God of his father now is his God. He has suddenly moved from not knowing God, to knowing God.

Yahweh gave Jacob promises that fulfilled Isaac's blessing. The promises confirmed his newly gained birthright, land, descendents, and God's presence—God's keeping power and future homecoming.

Jacob awoke from the dream and named the place where he slept Bethel, the house of God. He took the stone that was his pillow and anointed it with oil to create a sanctuary. The stain of the oil allowed others who traveled after him to recognize its significance. He established a place of worship even though he knew Yahweh would be with him wherever he went.

Unbelievable! It looks like the scoundrel has gotten away with the mother inspired scheme to defraud his father and brother. He remained God's chosen in spite of his "bad boy" ways.

Malcolm had a lot of "bad boy" ways. He took money out of his mother's wallet when she wasn't looking. He tortured his little sister with taunts about things she could not change—like her size. He even sold her cat's litter of kittens and pocketed the money. He wrecked the family car so many times that his father refused to let him drive it anymore. His mother often cried in my office over her son's behavior.

Malcolm "borrowed" his father's car one night while his parents were asleep to take his girlfriend to a club. On the way home in the predawn hours of the morning, he sideswiped a car as he left a parking lot. He left the scene of the accident without leaving the owner, who was still inside the club, with his name, address or insurance information.

The next day, when his father discovered the busted fender and headlight, Malcolm claimed he didn't know anything about it. His father inquired around the neighborhood. He was happily surprised when the next door neighbor, Mr. Wilson, said it was his car that had been hit. Appaently, Malcolm was not involved in the accident. This last lie bothered Malcolm. It gnawed at him. It plagued his mind. It disturbed him so much that a few days later, he blurted out to his father that he was the one who damaged the car.

Father and son stood looking at each other. The only sound in the room was the tick, tick, ticking of the clock on the wall. Finally his father said, I know.

Malcolm hugged his father for the first time in a long time. His father then gave him a list of things his mother needed from the grocery store. He told Malcolm to go pick up what was needed. When he returned, they would work on the plan to pay Mr. Wilson back.

It was an amazing moment of grace. Malcolm's father gave him another chance. It is also amazing that God gave Jacob another chance. God included Jacob, a liar, a cheat and a trickster who took advantage of a father in failing health. If God can include Jacob and all his dirty laundry, extend grace and a future undeserving, than God can also include us.

Destiny convinced herself that she didn't deserve God's blessings. In her mother's rigid world, she was a droid who was to follow instructions. She had no independent thoughts or actions of her own.

At the age of 14, she ran away from a controlling home environment. Her mother wanted her to stay in school and she wanted to stay in the streets. Her mother wanted her to learn to take responsibility for her education and she wanted to take responsibility for fun.

Life on the streets wasn't what she imagined. Destiny quickly became disillusioned. Rev. Barbara Brown Taylor writes that disillusion is the loss of illusion we have about ourselves, the world, God, family, friends, country and church. It is like living in fantasy land where no one is amused. She writes that it is not always a bad thing to lose the lies one has mistaken for truth.

One night at a house party, the high of choice was to take a handful of pills from a large bowl on the table. The pills weren't identified, but Destiny recognized a few uppers, downers and illegal pharmaceuticals.

It was a game. Everyone took turns grabbing pills and washing them down with beer. It was a game she decided to play.

When she woke up, she had no clothes, no wallet, no money or memory of what happened. Beside her laid a naked man who stared at her with wild glassy eyes. She tried to get up but he had her hands handcuffed to the bed.

She stopped counting the number of days she spent in that bed as his play toy. It was only when her body was covered with welts and her vagina battered and bleeding from his sadistic actions that he let her go.

Destiny was sick for days. She slept in hallways and alleys. One day, she stumbled into the Mission House downtown near the Inner Harbor. The mission workers got her medical attention, food and clothes. She didn't want to hear about the love of Jesus. She felt nothing but shame.

She never went home but stayed on the streets. She solicited to keep herself housed, fed and alive.

I met her during the first of three street revivals, called "Take Back the Streets" summer campaigns. The revivals were held near my church, Payne Memorial; Metropolitan United Methodist Church, Rev. Jeremiah Williams, pastor; and finally at Agape AME Church, pastored by the late Rev. Eleanor Bryant Graham.

Destiny, skimpily dressed, stood away from the service but on the fringes of the tent. Her "I don't really care" attitude began to crumble as the setting sun deepened the shadows on the sidewalk and the sky deepened from purple to a blue black, disappearing above the day glow of the street lights.

In the waning moments of the altar call, Destiny began to tremble uncontrollably. The revivalist threw out the gospel net. Destiny slowly walked forward on her three inch heels.

Tears rolled down her face, caking her thick pancake makeup. As she approached the makeshift altar, she sobbed loudly that Jesus couldn't possibly love her or forgive her of her sins. She didn't deserve salvation.

Thanks be to God that God doesn't give us what we deserve! God gives us what we need. I shared with her that when we confess our sins, God is faithful to forgive. We prayed the prayer of salvation together.

In the midst of Destiny's sobbing, old things passed away and behold she became a new Destiny. Now it was time for Destiny to forgive herself.

Destiny had to learn that forgiving herself would be a necessary and, possibly, a long process. She would need to begin her journey by taking steps to learn that she has value and worth—even in spite of what she had done or what someone else had done to her. Like Destiny, we all must stop trying to change our unchangeable past and forecasting our future behaviors.

Destiny's life had been controlled by abusive pimps and perverted johns long enough. It was time for her to trust God with her future. On that hot summer evening, with help, Destiny took the first step to walk away from an abusive street life into a new life filled with hope. She found a relationship with a Christ who saw her, pursued her, knew her and loved her without misusing her.

We may not have a testimony like Destiny but we may have controlling people or things in our lives that intimidate us into doing what they want us to do; destroy things that are important to us; will not allow us to speak or stop speaking to us for long periods of time; or trick us into believing what is not true about ourselves, simply to control us.

Destiny and Jacob had less than perfect beginnings. Jacob wrestled in the womb with his brother Esau and over his birthright and blessing. Destiny wrestled for control over her own life—at home and on the streets of Baltimore.

Each of them had a divine encounter that changed their expectations for the future. Each came to trust God for tomorrow.

Ralph Waldo Emerson wrote that "people are what their mothers make them." In some family units, patterns of behavior can be inherited.

Abusive behavior can be passed down from one generation to the next as if it were written in a Last Will and Testament. Children who live in conflict may grow to distrust the actions of those in and outside their family unit. In the midst of neglect, children may grow to believe that their needs are not important or develop a lack of their own self-worth. In an intense controlling environment, children may live under pressure to adhere to ridged expectations. The physical needs of a child might be provided but their emotional needs are neglected by parents who are over involved in themselves, work, church or a hobby.

Some of us had healthy childhoods. We were blessed to grow up in nurturing atmospheres where we received the appropriate emotional, physical, and spiritual support. We trusted our environment, learned to express our feelings, had our needs reasonably met, and formed satisfying relationships as adults.

On the other hand, some of us grow up in environments like Destiny's. We are caught in the crossfire of adults who say one thing but do another. There are families where children are exploited. Children are seen as disposable products and are used to meet the needs of adults.

Would you allow a two year old to smoke weed? Well, a family friend of a single mother thought it would be funny to see how the two year old boy would respond to the intoxicating and dangerous substance. No one would have known had the incident not been videotaped.

Some people came into this world like Jacob and Esau. They were in a struggle before birth or were born with something holding their heel. The struggle is something that isn't strong enough to impede the birthing process but it can be something that trips us up later in life. Crack babies and children born with fetal alcohol syndrome have been grabbed by the heel because of these maladies.

Emerson's quote may or may not be true. What is true is that God can bless you to live long enough to see adulthood. When you leave home, you take your childhood with you. This includes the ups and downs, ins and outs, the good, the wonderful, and the ugly. You may not leave your family or problems behind. History might repeat itself, as there is a desire to "normalize" negative experiences or create a "reality" that is normal. Familiarity is comforting even if it is negative.

What you will gain when you leave home is an opportunity to perpetuate the positive and change the negative. You don't need your parent's permission to change. You become the initiator of change. What is true is that we are who God says we are. We are fearfully and wonderfully made in the image of God. In Christ, old things pass away and a new life is gained, transformed by the saving sacrificial love of Christ.

The Counseling Center at the University of Illinois suggests that change begins by identifying difficult or painful experiences that happened during childhood. Make a list of behaviors that you would like to change such as when you used abusive language. Include yelling at your children or beliefs such as "I deserved it" or "I had it coming because" I was a rotten child. Make a companion list of the behaviors or beliefs that you would like to exhibit. Pick a behavior to change and choose the alternate appropriate behavior to exhibit. Once you have learned a new positive way to communicate and/or act, go to the next item on your list.

Change happens over time; not over night. Be patient. Change is often one step ahead and two steps back. Don't be discouraged to start all over again to build the life you desire to live. If you need professional help to do it or get through it, seek the appropriate care and get it!

The Center advises that you are not in control of the lives of other people and you do not have the power to change other people. Obviously, Rebekah and Jacob did not read their "Understanding Dysfunctional Relationship Patterns in Your Family." Their deceptive plan tried to control the outcome of destiny.

In 2 Kings 6–8, we find another occasion where the issue of control rises to the surface. Israel is a divided nation. The northernmost area is Israel and the southernmost area is Judah.

The prophet Elijah was in heaven and the mantle of leadership now fell to Elisha. The important task of succession of leadership was complete. Success without succession could be considered a failure.

Just as Rebekah was concerned about who would receive the birthright and God's blessing, God is also concerned about what family would inherit the next generation of leadership. God does not prepare the next generation in a vacuum, but prepares the future in the presence of the present.

Elijah was prepared in the sight of Elisha. Joshua was prepared in the sight of Moses. Samuel was prepared in the sight of Eli. The disciples were prepared in the presence of Jesus.

Oftentimes, we are so busy with our own agendas that we neglect to see signs of the future. If we understood how God prepares the next level of leadership, we would not be as hostile to the "wannabes" around us. You know how we can act. We are afraid to lose control of the business, classroom, ministry, friends or family because others show potential. We are afraid that others will steal our thunder, our stuff, our spotlight, our position, our company, or our ideas.

How will the Joshua generation learn if the Moses generation is not willing to teach them? Ignore them now and they will ignore you when they get into the driver's seat. Teach, train, mentor and leave a lasting legacy by planting seeds into the lives of the next generation that will grow and prosper.

Elisha had another encounter with a Shunnamite woman. The prophet had at one time stayed with the well-to-do woman and her husband in Shunnum. She was barren. It was something beyond her control.

God caused her womb to open and prosper. She gave birth to a son but the boy got sick. It too was something beyond her control. The boy died. God, however, intervened through the prophet and life was restored to the boy.

In the eighth chapter, Elisha again instructed the woman that something would happen that would be beyond her control. Over the next seven years, God would cause a famine to engulf the land. She was instructed to take her family and move wherever she could find shelter.

There were no moving vans provided, no boxes to pack her belongings, no transportation funds in the budget, no departure party, and no one to welcome her on the other end. She just had to go. She left and stayed in the land of the Philistines.

At the end of the famine, she returned home. The Shunnamite woman went to the ruler to beg for the return of the house and land she willingly had left behind. He just happened to be talking to Gehazi, Elisha's servant, about the great things the prophet had done.

Just as Gehazi was telling the ruler about how Elisha restored the life of a dead boy, the Shunnamite woman walked in. The servant Gehazi said, "This is the woman and this is her son."

The Shunnamite woman told the ruler what God had done for her when things were beyond her control.

"Give back everything that belonged to her," said the ruler, "including the income from the land, from the day she left the country until now."

There are three specific ways in which the Shunnamite woman had no control over her life. First, she could not have children—she was barren. Her body was out of her control. This was a personal attack on her.

Second, her son became ill and died—she could not save her son's life. She had no control over her son's well-being. Sometimes, bad things can happen to those close to you. Rebekah finally went to Isaac because Esau had threatened to kill Jacob. This is an example of when things are out of control in a family.

Third, her livelihood was threatened by famine—she could not control her surroundings. She had no control over the environment. It wasn't an attack on her or her loved ones but on where she lived.

What impresses me about this woman is her source of strength. Her relationship with God made the difference. Rebekah believed what God said to her in the oracle. Jacob did not have a relationship with the God of his father until he was caught in the cross hairs of his own devious activities.

The Shunnamite woman's source of strength is found in her connection to God. Her love of God led her to provide for God's prophet. She sought nothing for herself. This was not a situation of, "If I do for you, you do for me." "If I scratch your back, you scratch mine." No, she gave without looking for something in return.

She prepared a proper place for the prophet to stay, a room furnished and set apart so whenever the prophet was in town, he had a place to stay. Her love for God showed in her ministry of hospitality. Although her body was beyond her control, her love and her level of service did not diminish because of this. She did not use her body as an excuse to exempt her from life's responsibilities. She didn't allow her situation to handicap her. It enabled her to hold up and hold out when everything within her and around her were beyond her control.

We need to find our strength in our connection with God. As our grandmothers sang, "Like a tree planted by the waters I shall not be moved." Or "I've been 'buked and I've been scorned. I've been talked about sures you born." And "I ain't gwine ta lay my 'legion down."

It was her relationship with God that helped her to carry on when her only son had died. The God you call on when there is an unexpected bend in the road is the creator of all things. She learned that God was more than the creator but also the sustainer of life.

In the daily rush of our own living, it is easy to lose our connection. Life is on the line. God is calling and we fail to click the call waiting button because we want to handle it ourselves. In the end, we fail to make the connection. We lose the call or simply live beyond our call service area.

If we are not careful, we will lose our connection with our source of strength—the source that helps us endure depressions and disappointments, helps us cancel our pity parties, and allows us to be blessed with abundant life.

Do not get caught off guard by God's unexpected blessings. God is always doing the unexpected. The Shunnamite woman trusted God with the outcome. In order to trust God with the results, you have to stop trying to control the results. Release the need to control. Take your hands off the issue. You may be the one holding back your blessing because you are in God's way. You are not in control.

In everything that happened to the Shunnamite woman, she never stopped trusting God. Her son got sick but she never stopped trusting God. Her son died but she never stopped trusting God. Her community was in crises. She had to leave all she ever knew. She came home with no guarantee that the house or land she left would be restored. Still, she never stopped trusting God.

It is easy to trust God when things are going as planned. Trust is always easy to do when the expected happens according to your predictable order.

If for whatever reason, you awake feeling outnumbered, outgunned, overwhelmed and about to break under the pressure of another problem, trust God. If you already prayed to God asking protection from one more problem, one more mistake, one more misunderstanding, mess up, rejection, miscarriage, death, transfer—continue to trust in God. Most of the things that happen to us are beyond your control—trust God!

The Shunnamite woman found the strength to carry on from her relationship with God. She stayed connected. She trusted God to handle what she could not handle. When she came back, her house was restored. Her lands were restored. She missed no paydays and the income that her land had earned was restored to her.

Finally, it may be beyond your control but it is never beyond the control of God. The woman learned that God was more than a predictor of future events. God is more than a creator, a sustainer, and healer. God has the power to get your stuff back—even when we volunteer to walk away from our stuff. Sometimes we are willing to walk away from jobs, marriages, children, relationships, and careers—not because God directed it but because of reasons only known to us.

This woman had the faith to believe that God is able to recover what is lost. Further, she had faith to depend on God, not on herself; her intellect, her economic status, her skills, her paychecks, or past experiences.

She was able to see the hand of God behind every event and saw that God had the last word!

Many of us go through life afraid of what tomorrow might bring or that the events of tomorrow might not work out like we planned. We become fearful that we will not be liked, we will not be accepted, we will never belong to anyone, we will not make enough money, we will not be successful, we will be poor parents or neglectful spouses.

We turn ourselves into manipulating mavens afraid that we will never arrive or never cross the finish line, get AIDS, die of cancer, go to war, make a fool of ourselves, or fail a course or the exam. We are afraid that we will get to the end of the road and look back only to realize that we have taken the wrong road on someone else's say so.

When God is in control—and God is in control—God will restore the years that the locust had eaten away; will bring to life, old dead wombs; heal the sick and raise the dead; retrieve lost peace; give back stolen seasons and sanity. God has the power to get our stuff back because God has the last word.

When God has the last word, mess turns into miracles and mistakes into lessons learned. Problems become possibilities and crises turn into stepping stones. Hardships become character builders, trials become triumphs, and tragedies become testimonies.

God will take a prostitute and turn her into an evangelist like the woman at the well. God can take a pregnant teenage mother and turn her into the earthly mother of god. God can take Rahab, an innkeeper who was a whore, and put her into faith's hall of fame. And God can turn a murderer into a missionary like Paul. God can take the cross, a symbol of death, violence, degradation and shame, and turn it into an instrument of salvation. How you might ask? Because God has the last word!

I am not sure who this word is for but the doctor does not have the last word; the lawyer does not have the last word; the judge does not have the last word; the chairman of the board does not have the last word; your mother does not have the last word; your father does not have the last word; your friends do not have the last word; network TV executives, the bank executive, nor your employer have the last word.

It looked like the trickster Jacob was doomed but God had the last word. In the years to come the proverbial "what goes around comes around" would play itself during Jacob's years with his Uncle Laban. In the midst of deception, God was still working out the promises made to Jacob's ancestors. God had the last word.

S.M.A.R.T MOVES
(Spiritual Motivation for Action and Real Transformation)

Talking Points

1. Do you always like to be in control of everything and everybody?
2. Do you control your spouse or significant other with intimidation, isolation or verbal abuse?
3. Has anyone ever told you that all the problems in your relationship are your fault?
4. Have you ever thought you lived beyond God's grace; not deserving of salvation?
5. In what ways did you experience manipulative personalities in your childhood?
6. What aspects of your childhood did you take with you when you left home?
7. Have you forgiven your parent/parents for an imperfect childhood or childhood environment?
8. Have you been able to forgive yourself for past mistakes?
9. Have you forgiven others for past afflictions?

The Word of Prayer

Let us pray:

Dear God, in the quietness of this moment, I confess that I have tried to wrestle the control of my life and the lives of others from your hand. Forgive me for not trusting the plans that you have for me, plans not to harm but prosper me. I resign from trying to be God all by myself. I release my past, my present and my future into your hands. In Jesus' Name, Amen.

Today, ask God to help you to respect yourself and others so that you do not hurt anyone with your words or deeds.

The Word of God

"Trust the Lord with all your heart and lean not unto your own understanding." (Proverbs 3:5–6)

"I will praise you, O Lord, with all my heart; I will tell of your wonder. I will be glad and rejoice in you; I will sing praises to your name, O Lord Most High." (Psalm 91:1–2)

Foreplay

Today, choose a negative behavior that you need to change. For example, if you yell at your children, spouse, lover or friends, gain control of your anger by choosing an alternate behavior. Try taking deep breaths. Count to ten before you speak. Think before you speak. Stick a pin in it and come back to it when you are calm.

Aunt Agony suggests that you try watching *Divorce Court* and consider Judge Lynn Toler's Smith-and-Wesson test. If you think you can't stop something, ask yourself, would you be able to do it if someone held a Smith and Wesson to your head? If the answer is yes, than the problem is not ability but motivation.

Pillow Talk

Look for the "hidden pearls" in your childhood. "Hidden pearls" are what Gary Smalley calls the hidden positives in a negative experience or priceless pearls from the sandstorms of life.

Aunt Agony would disclose to you that her mother had an ironing cord problem. Whenever she disciplined one of her seven kids, she would detach the cord from the iron—that was in the days when irons had detachable cords. Her mother used it as a switch on the back of her legs and buttocks.

"I was scared for life," said Aunt Agony. What is her hidden pearl? She never learned how to iron clothes because of her fear of the ironing cord.

"It is hazardous to my health," she says. "That's my story and I'm sticking to it!"

Kiss and Tell

Bring your right hand up to your lips and give yourself a kiss. Give yourself a hug. Now tell yourself: "I will not let myself be limited by my past!"

Kiss and Makeup

Parents and spouses are people too. They may have been incapable of creating a nurturing, loving and supportive environment. You can remain twisted in knots by the past or launch onto the sea of forgiveness. Forgiveness means releasing the offender. You untie yourself from the people and events that have hurt you.

Look in the mirror and say out loud: "I forgive you! I untie the emotional ropes that have held me down. It is not my fault. I am not responsible for your wounds. I will not allow your offensive behavior to ruin the rest of my life! I forgive you!" Remember, some things happen over time, not overnight.

Marital Madness

It is madness to make your spouse pay for something someone else did to you. Since you may not be able to express how you feel to those who hurt you in the past, you prefer to take your anger out on your spouse or significant other.

It is also madness to keep the gates of your heart of hearts closed because you are afraid to let those who are close to you to do further damage.

Singularity

Destiny felt she was unworthy of God's love. At first she felt so unworthy she had a hard time dating. She believed that if she fell in love and her sordid past was revealed, she'd be rejected.

Avoid trying to predict the future by past experiences. You are so important that Jesus died so you could have an abundant life. Today, take one step to grow to a new beginning. The past cannot be changed but you and God can create a new future.

TWO

LOVE AT FIRST SIGHT

Then Jacob kissed Rachel and began to weep aloud.

Genesis 29:11

Love at first sight is easy to understand;
it's when two people have been looking at each other
for a lifetime that it becomes a miracle.

Amy Bloom

Sitting in the kitchen on a Sunday evening, our two young adult daughters asked me, "What did Dad bring to the table during your relationship?" Startled by the question I responded as any mother would, "Huh!"

"What did Dad have to offer?" asked the older of the two.

The answer to the question quickly ran through my mind and I immediately began to filter out the ones that mothers do not discuss with their twenty-something single daughters.

"Well," I began tentatively, "He was tall, dark and handsome. He wasn't the kind of professional athlete who was stuck on himself. He was able to include me in his world and I was able to include him in mine."

"Come on Mom," said the oldest again. "Tell us the truth. What did he give you that you didn't already have? How else will we ever find a husband?"

There are women and men in this world who hope, wish and pray for a "happily ever after" relationship. They are secretly, quietly or openly analyzing every touch, text message or lingering look from the opposite sex. They wonder about every hug that's held a little bit longer than all the others. When the pulse rate goes up and the heart flutters, is this lust or love?

In this new relational world, women must navigate the treacherous waters of men who are on the down low or otherwise connected to other women. On the other hand, men must weed out the women who are not looking for love but a meal ticket and a new wardrobe.

If men and women are looking for quality relationships that end in covenant coupling, then how come getting together is so hard?

In this chapter, we will take a look at love at first sight, looking for the right one in the right places, as well as Aunt Agony's guidance on kissing.

Relationships can be as easy as holding hands or as complicated as docking a space shuttle to a space station, thousands of miles above the earth.

Cynthia walked into my office one morning declaring that she would never fall in love again. She felt that falling meant the possibility of hitting the ground. She was tired of traumatic breakups or hitting the ground face first. Next time, she insisted, she would "walk" in love, "stroll" in love, but never "fall" in love again. Love and marriage may go together like "a horse and carriage," lettuce and tomatoes, peas and carrots, and bread and butter. As an insurance company ad goes, however, "Life comes at you fast."

Relationships can bring out the best or the worst in us. Dannella loved Rashid. It didn't matter that Rashid didn't love her back. She knew it was just a matter of time before he would come around and see that she was the one for him. She sent him daily e-mails and text messaged him on holidays. She took photos of him and posted them on her "Face Book" web page.

When Rashid failed to respond to her attempts to woo him, she stalked him at work and at home. She confronted him in public places, making more than one scene in front of friends and family. She was obsessed. No amount of gentle persuasion would change her mind.

One night, her pursuit of happiness ended when she got angry after he refused to invite her into his home. First, she broke out the windows in his car, and then she got in the expensive foreign automobile and defecated in the driver's seat. The arresting officer struggled to take her into custody.

Karen, on the other hand, lived a selfish sheltered suburban life. Her world was defined by her wants to the exclusion of the needs of others. Her days were filled with mall wonderings and on-line shopping. She had made out her "To Be" list a long time ago. Her dream man had "to be" rich, "to be" employed, "to be" famous, "to be" tall, "to be" handsome, "to be" intelligent, "to be" physically fit, and "to be" attentive to her every need.

The list fell apart when Bernard came along. The only category he matched on her list was the "to be" employed.

They met at the mall where he worked at a kiosk for a nonprofit organization. He sold products that helped to support a group home for unwed teens. A group home and poor unwed teens was a world far different from Karen's comfortable life. He gradually pulled her into a new world that reconnected her to her most intimate self—a place far from her superficial pursuit of happiness. She soon began to reach beyond herself to help young girls get back on their feet.

Bernard met his match when he fell in love with Karen. She helped him look beyond his pursuit of success and achievements and exposed him to new forms of exciting experiences he didn't want to end.

Angel was a marriage wannabe. She wanted to be married. She read bridal magazines, went to bridal shows, planned her honeymoon and picked her negligee for her wedding night—even though she had no prospects in sight.

Angel entered every relationship with marriage in mind. She said yes to Paul, the first man who proposed to her. The problem, however, concerned the enormous amount of time that was spent planning the wedding ceremony while basically no time was spent discussing how to make their marriage succeed *after* the ceremony. They were in love with the idea of *getting* married more than they were in *being* married.

Relationships can take our emotions on a wild journey. It can be intimate, beautiful, and adventurous. It can also be a dangerous expedition filled with traps, tricks and dead end trails.

We want to be in relationship heaven but instead of going out with friends, we stay home and make it a Blockbuster night. We text message each other more than we talk to each other face to face. All night long, we chat online with people we don't know more than we talk with the people with whom we live.

A radio talk show host was asked what he believed to be the best thing about being married. He answered that there was someone to come home to. When asked what was the worst thing about his marriage, he answered that there was someone to come home to.

We want stronger relationships yet we watch television in separate rooms. Contractors are building new homes with two master bedrooms, predicting that this will be the sleeping arrangement of 21st century couples. And it has nothing to do with sex!

Mary Pipher, in *The Shelter of Each Other*, concludes that with more, we have less. There is more sexual information and stimulation available but we are not happy. There are more forms of entertainment, yet we are still bored. People grow emotionally numb in a culture that is focused on feelings. We have less time but more time-saving gadgets. There are more books available with fewer readers, and more information among a growing number of uninformed people. We are a nation of people who hunger for values, community and something to which we can dedicate ourselves, yet we don't go to church. Likewise, we long for personal connections, yet we find ourselves isolated from each other.

Our pursuit of relational happiness has led us in the opposite direction from where we really want to go. It is filled with ironies and contradictions.

Pipher calls it a crisis of meaning. The cultural climate makes it hard for families to be happy because, among other things, we have learned that products solve problems. Other social commentators have said that there is a culture of consumption that is leading us toward profound disappointment. We end up like the Lone Ranger—but without Tonto.

My husband Stan and I participated in that circular want more, get less pattern of living. We wanted more time with each other but got less. We wanted more time for family and friends but got less. We wanted more time for slow walks because the demands of work and ministry did not provide us with enough time for each other.

We finally came to the conclusion that what we needed was a night dedicated only to us. This would be our "date night." Our kids were astonished. They couldn't understand why married people needed a "date night." Dates are the discovery channel of relationships. No matter how long you have been together, there is still something new to discover or something to rediscover about each other.

Perhaps I am a true example of my Baby Boomer generation. A date is something that involves spending time with someone over dinner, watching a movie, or dancing at a party. It is a "just us" time to do something or nothing together. It is done beyond the listening ears of children and the prying eyes of in-laws. More importantly, it is distinguishable from boy's night out and girl's night out.

Relationships have evolved over time. We have gone from 17th and 18th century matchmakers to the Lonely Hearts Club to personal ads. Today, dates are arranged by companies that put busy professionals together in an interview format. Their key advertising lingo is, "It's not a commitment, it's just lunch."

Spending time together in exploratory conversation has turned into Speed Dating sponsored by restaurants, bars and radio stations. A person gets five to ten minutes of face time across a table. When the time is up, they move to the next person to see if anything clicks. It is barely enough time to exchange names and e-mails. Call backs are made based on superficial information. It is all about what the person looks and sounds like and the gut reaction to the ten minute interview.

Speed Dating has gone upscale. Only the rich and beautiful are invited to this event. Photographs and financial statements are reviewed in advance. Once you have passed the screening process, there is an opportunity for rich men to meet beautiful women and rich women to meet handsome men.

The internet's eHarmony dating company takes a different approach to matchmaking. They utilize a survey that identifies whether two people are compatible based on a set of likes and dislikes. One of my daughters actually knows a couple who met through this process. They went through a season of on-again, off-again dating but have been married with children for three years.

I asked Aunt Agony how she felt about speed dating. "Speed dating," she said. "I would if there was a skating rink nearby."

"Aunt Agony it's speed dating not speed skating!" I replied.

"Sweetie, you must forgive me. Sometimes my bun is too tight and all the blood drains from by brain. Once back in 1952, I was moving pretty fast. We didn't call it speed dating back then. It was called relationship roulette. You knew that the gun was loaded but you weren't sure when it would go off!"

"It wouldn't hurt to slow down when it comes to men. Some things need time like good wine, cheese, pot roast and slow roasted Columbian coffee. Otherwise, hun, you'll end up with a jack-in-the-box."

"What's a jack-in-the-box? You mean a hamburger," I said.

"No, it's a clown who jumps out of his box with too many surprises: kids, wife, sumthin' on the side or connected to sumthin' hazardous to your health!"

Jacob engaged in a centuries old style of speed dating. It's called love at first sight. He came, he saw, and he conquered.

Jacob continued on his eastward journey from Beersheba to Haran. He approached a well in the middle of a field where shepherds began to arrive with their herds. He immediately became embroiled in a water rights issue.

Jacob learned that the men are from Haran and inquired about his Uncle Laban, Nahor's grandson. They indicated that his uncle was well and pointed out his uncle's daughter, a shepherdess by the name of Rachel.

Rachel could not water her sheep because the sun was too high and all the shepherds had not gathered at the well. The community water rights system was simple. A large stone covered the mouth of the well. It was so large that it took all of the shepherds to move it. It was assured then that no one took more than their fair share of the water.

Jacob is impatient. He does not want to wait until the shepherd community has gathered. He ignored the community custom and moved the stone for Rachel to water her flock. In that moment, he elevated himself above the local tradition, demonstrating that he had both authority and great physical strength.

No words were spoken. No formal greeting was given. No introductions were made. There was no matchmaker present or speed dating event scheduled at the well.

Jacob kissed Rachel and wept aloud. (That must have been some kiss!)

There must have been something about wells and falling in love. Moses met Zipporah at the well. They got married. Isaac met Rebekah at the spring with her jar. They married. Now Jacob kisses Rachael, a virtual stranger at a well.

These three couples are not the only ones to fall in love at first sight. There's William Shakespeare's Romeo and Juliet and Victor Hugo's Marius Pontmercy and Cosette in *Les Miserables*.

The Greco-Roman interpretation of love at first sight focused on the eyes. The eyes of the beautiful loved object were like arrows that shot directly into a person's eyes. The arrows would travel to the heart of the would-be lover. The heart would be overwhelmed by longings and yearnings for the beautiful loved object. If the love was returned, desire was requited. If not, depression would engulf the castoff.

Some of us are hopeless romantics. How can you tell? You can run quickly through a growing list of chick flicks or the overwhelming number of romance novels that are published each year. There are many women whose minds are captured and held hostage by childhood visions of the handsome prince who will come into their lives. With one look, the dashing prince would recognize that they were the person with whom he cannot live without and they would ride off into the sunset of marital bliss.

This is what I affectionately call the "Cinderella Syndrome." This is the state of mind that says, no matter how evil the times, no matter how evil the stepmother or stepsisters or how many tricks they use to keep you away from the ball, the prince will still be able to find his princess. He will use his satellite global positioning mechanism to locate you even if you are wearing knock-off designer rags while you scrub floors and haul coal. He could also find you even if you were living in an attic and only talked to your live-in mouse and the visiting bluebirds! The king will be able to find his queen and the prince his princess!

While daydreaming as little girls, some of you may have played the stolen beauty game. This is what I call the Maid Marian disorder. It is a "kidnap and rescue" scenario. You are the beautiful young ward of an important man, the king, who is constantly away on business. You are kidnapped by a rogue who turns out to be a good guy and you fall in love with him.

You are again kidnapped by someone who is supposed to be the good guy but is really the bad guy, the evil brother of the king. You are forced to marry him. Are you keeping up? You are rescued from a very bad marriage to the evil brother just in time to marry the rogue who has won your heart.

All of us want to be desired. We want that someone who loves us to pursue us like Nathaniel pursued Cora in *The Last of the Mohicans*. He declared that he would find her no matter how far he had to go or how long it would take.

Trust me, women are not hanging around waiting to be taken like Helen of Troy. We do yearn to be in a relationship and to be a part of something good. It is so valuable that many believe it is worth spending their life making it work and keeping it real. As Diana Ross' character

Tracy said to Billie Dee Williams' Brian, her politician boyfriend in *Lady Sings the Blues*, "What good is success without sharing it with someone?"

I asked Aunt Agony had she ever dreamed about being rescued by a handsome man.

"Why of course sweetie. I dream every night of being rescued by Denzel Washington. But when I wake up in the morning, I'm still with Fred Sanford in the junkyard," she said.

In our minds, we can always work out our fantasies. It is best not to let them mingle with your own reality show or real life and love. Anais Nin states that we have all been poisoned by fairytales.

Scientists are now saying that love at first sight is quite possible. In a study in the *Journal of Social and Personal Relationships*, they concluded that in only a few minutes people decide whether to dump or keep their date even before the appetizers arrive. All it takes is ten minutes.

Artemia Ramire, one of the report's coauthors, suggests that people do not want to waste time. Speed dating has value because it becomes a self-fulfilling prophecy. People make a prediction about what kind of relationship they could have with a person. The positive or negative response determines how much time and effort they put into getting to know the other person.

Aunt Agony said that she has fallen in love with a total stranger. She said, "I have fallen in love many times with a complete stranger and I still don't know who I am!"

Another report indicated that love at first sight depends on our state of mind at the time we meet someone. If we are stressed, depressed, in a hurry or preoccupied, we may not notice a person's eyes, radiant smile or charming wit. If we are open to new experiences or ready to invite others into our lives, we may notice something that rings our bell. This is when intuition, common sense, gut reaction and our ideals come into play.

Carl Jung theorizes that everyone develops ideal male and female soul mates as unconscious archetypes. When we meet someone who matches our archetype, that person awakens in us the sleeping ideal. Our response seems beyond our control. We believe we have met the man or woman of our dreams and they possess what we have been looking for all our lives.

Our archetype may include things like confidence, resourcefulness, protecting persona, kindness, sexy, unselfish or compassionate. We can fall in love instantly or faster than we ever realized.

In any case, Aunt Agony would tell you to look before you leap. "Keep your feet on the ground honey. If it is true love, enjoy the ride. If it is not, the ground can be tough on the buttocks. " In the words of A. W. Tozer, "Thirsty hearts are those whose longings have been wakened by the touch of God within then."

One of my daughters left home in the traditional college dorm regalia: jeans, tiny tee shirt, hair wrapped under a scarf, topped off with a Von Dutch hat. Visit any college campus and you will wonder if young women have heard of the "just one look" possibility.

I reminded her that she could meet her future husband at the mall—the equivalency of the well in the middle of the field—while dressed like that. She agreed with me and said that her future husband would probably have on the same thing, scarf and all!

There are many women and men who are secretly, quietly, knowingly, and openly waiting for their future soul-mate to walk in the door. They are waiting for someone who sees their competencies as assets, not liabilities. They are waiting for someone who is not threatened by their intellect—whether it is affirmed or unaffirmed by college degrees.

Sisters are waiting for that someone who is not threatened by their efficiency or overwhelmed by their moral character. They are yearning for that special someone who is not embarrassed by their faith in Jesus Christ or afraid of their devotion to God, church and community.

One Monday evening at a Circle of Love meeting, I asked Rhonda what kind of man she was waiting for. She said she was looking for someone with whom she could lay a foundation of trust, respect, and emotional intimacy. On this type of foundation and with the right person, she believed she could build a forever love relationship.

The Circle of Love, held bimonthly on Monday evenings, was a women's fellowship ministry at two of my former churches, Oak Street AME Church and Payne Memorial AME Church in Baltimore, Maryland. At the Circle of Love meetings, we often talked about love and marriage. The Circle was a place to share life's daily struggles in a protective environment. Women sought Biblical answers for everyday questions. Those Monday nights were special. It was a brief respite from the whirlwind of love, marriage, motherhood, friendships and careers.

Rhonda said she was not looking for someone who was married to anyone else, seeing anyone else, or looking to see someone on the side. She wanted a man who was not married to their job. She didn't want someone who pretended to be single or pretended to be separated from his wife while he waited for her to sign the divorce papers. She also didn't want someone who was in town on a business trip and looking for a good time or someone who wanted to stay married just because of the kids.

"I learned a long time ago that you get what you're looking for," she said. "You are the one in charge of the quality of your life."

There are several theories about how we ultimately select the "right man or woman." One theory indicates that we select prospective spouses by identifying those who are our equals. In our "hunt and hit-on" process, we evaluate the other with the kind of strategy that goes into making a business partnership or acquisition. When we conclude that they have enough points to win the game, we allow them to score.

Another theory is based on basic biology. We choose who we choose based on unconscious selections of the survival of the fittest. Males are drawn to those who project a picture of beauty and health, indicating they are ripe for procreation. Females make decisions based on the male's ability to protect and provide, irrespective of their age. If their "alpha" behavior traits, such as dominance or strength, indicate that they can best other males, the female will settle with that male.

The third theory is not based on psychology or biology. It is based on one's persona. This theory states that we look for someone who enhances our self image. We look for the one who basically makes us look good.

According to Dr. Harville Hendrix, in *Getting the Love You Want*, these theories are still inadequate. We tend to be attracted to people who have a particular set of positive and negative personality packages. Without realizing it, we tend to be drawn to the same type of person with the same type of character traits.

Whoever thought that looking for the right person in the right place could be so difficult?

In Luke 2:36–40, Anna the prophetess was also waiting for the right man to come along. Luke wants us to know Jesus as a universal Messiah. Jesus is the one who breaks down social and cultural barriers and jumps over prejudicial and exclusionary philosophies. He risks his status and purity to talk to women as well as touch the diseased and impoverished. He took the side of the beleaguered who occupied the lowest rungs of the socioeconomic ladder.

In this pericope, Luke pairs Anna with Simeon in the temple at the end of the birth narrative. Anna is waiting.

Anna is a prophet, the first female prophet revealed in the New Testament. She joins her old covenant sisters, Miriam, Deborah and Huldah. She is perhaps between eighty and eighty-four years of age. She married at an early age but after seven years of marriage, her husband died.

Night and day, Anna was in the temple in Jerusalem fasting, praying and worshipping God. She established a consistent spiritual discipline that placed her in a solid religious posture. When others had come and gone, Anna was still at the temple. During festival time or peak worship hours, Anna was there. When the church was crowded, Anna was in her place. If no one showed up, she was still there.

The Mosaic Law required the purification of the mother after the birth of a child. The normal physiological process of birth and menses somehow disqualified and tainted a woman's worship relationship with God.

Mary and Joseph took the baby Jesus to the temple to fulfill what the law required. They made the appropriate sacrifices. In doing so, Simeon saw the young couple and child. He took Jesus in his arms and praised God.

It had been previously revealed to Simeon that he would not see death until he saw the Messiah. He sees the Christ child in the arms of his parents and praises God for such a blessing. Simeon can now die in peace.

In almost the same breath, Anna sees Jesus. Her words are not recorded but her presence is preserved. She too affirms the Christ and speaks about the child to those who are looking for the redemption of Jerusalem.

Anna was not waiting for a flesh and blood phenomenon. She was waiting for the Son of God. Anna certainly is in the right place at the right time. Her faith kept her in position until the "right" man came along. You can be in the right place and still do not know what you are looking for.

What I love about Anna and Rhonda is that their archetype was not weighed down with superficial concerns such as: Was he driving the right car? Did he own the right house? Did he have ample finances? Or was his hair kinky, straight or curly? What a person drives, wears or is able to own should not be the most important concern. Rhonda did not mention her ideal was based upon how broad, slim, solid, soft or sensual they were.

These physical perceptions can be so easily influenced by the media, which impacts our perception of reality.

Anna was in the right place to find the right person. She was fasting and praying. Prayer helps you to have the mindset of Christ and the heart of God.

Yet, we rarely pray about our deepest concerns. We prefer to face our relationship problems alone. I would be afraid to speed date, exchange telephone numbers or give my e-mail address to a stranger without first talking to God. We might understand the power of prayer but we still make decisions without first consulting God.

There are plaguing personal problems that cause us to set up permanent campsites in our lives. On one hand, deep down inside we believe God. But on the other hand, we do not believe that God has the power to handle our problems irrespective if we are or aren't in a loving relationship.

Reach out to God in prayer. God's loving arms are stretched in your direction and prayer touches the hands of God. In God's hands, we will find what we have been looking for. In prayer, God will identify our enemies and strategize our victories. God will tell us who to stay away from and who to draw closer to. God will warn you of impending danger and put back into your life what has been beaten out of your life.

Prayer is the pipeline that renews, restores and refreshes our spirit. Prayer is your confession that you are not in control of what other people may say about you.

Prayer is the time to adjust your attitude. If you hate your life, you will make it miserable for yourself and others. The Son of God will help you fall in love with life. Jesus says that he has come that you may have life and have it more abundantly. Falling in love with life is the pathway to falling in love with someone or staying in love with a spouse.

You can be in the right place, doing the right things, knowing what to look for and still miss Jesus. The rich young ruler was in the right place. He, however, became more concerned about his possessions than following Jesus and he missed a life transforming opportunity. Nine out of ten lepers failed to come back and thank Jesus for their healing. They missed an important opportunity. Judas was a member of the talented twelve disciples. Every day, he served Christ and traveled with him. Yet, Judas betrayed Jesus for thirty pieces of silver. He missed an important opportunity.

One day in the temple, there were perhaps hundreds of people. The priests were performing their temple rituals and responsibilities. The Pharisees were on duty and in charge. The Scribes were perhaps maintaining or adding to the written record. Only two people saw the Messiah that day. It only took one look for them to fall in love.

S.M.A.R.T. MOVES

(Spiritual Motivation for Action and Real Transformation)

Talking Points

1. Do you believe in love at first sight?

2. Have you ever been in love with love?

3. Are you waiting to be rescued by the man or woman of your dreams?

4. What fantasies or fairy tales from your childhood impact your relationships?

5. Write a Relational Ten Commandments. List ten "must haves" that represent your criteria for a person to pass the speed dating test. It could include things such as kindness, compassion, civic minded, loves children, stable, sophisticated or height, weight, career, financial status and other character traits.

The Word of Prayer

Open our eyes today that we may see how unfailing your love is towards us. Forgive us for being so busy that we neglected to look in your direction. Make us to know the depth of your love that heals our failures and shortcomings. Help us to be in right places doing right things in your name we pray, amen.

The Word of God

"Dear friend, let us love one another, for love comes from God. Everyone who loves has been born of God and knows God. Whoever does not love does not know God because God is love." (1 John 4:7–8)

"But I trust in your unfailing love; my heart rejoices in your salvation. I will sing to the Lord, for he has been good to me. " (Psalm 13:5–6)

Foreplay

Don't rush the goodbye kiss with your usual peck on the cheek or with a feather light brush of the lips that barely reach its mark. This morning kiss for REAL and mean it! If you are kissed, kiss back. There is no air kissing in Aunt Agony's world!

Pillow Talk

Tonight, after the game is over (football, basketball, baseball, or beach volleyball) and the kids are in bed, whisper the meaning for each kiss to your significant other. Pucker up and give a demonstration—do it quickly before they fall asleep or before they think that you have lost your mind (especially if you haven't done that in awhile).

Kiss and Tell

A real kiss puts intimacy in your day. Today, kiss those who you love and tell them something good: "I'm glad you're in my life."

Kiss and Make-Up

Everyone might not warm up to the kiss program right away. Every kiss might not make you cry like Jacob. Every smooch will not rival Fourth of July pyrotechnics. So don't let your feelings bruise so easily. Sometimes you may want to be close while your partner might want some distance. You can either slow your roll and gently wait them out or speak up about your desire to show your affection with a kiss. They may view this new interest in kissing as too close for comfort (smothering). Find the right balance that works for the two of you.

Marital Madness

If your significant other simply does not know how to kiss, do not disclose this information to him. Aunt Agony would never tell you to lie, but she will tell you that if you have nothing good to say, don't say anything at all! There is more than one way to skin a cat and you can teach an old dog to kiss!

Singularity

Aunt Agony would warn you, do not promise a kiss that you are not ready to deliver! Bait and switch* in the affairs of the heart is always frowned upon. Why, you might ask? Because you may end up being forced to give away what you can never get back—your virginity or your reputation. You can be labeled a tease.

*Bait and switch is when a person's kiss and body language suggests more than they really want to deliver. When the other person responds, the other suddenly switches to another less enticing mood. It's like turning off the hot to cold water.

THREE

TEMPORARY INSANITY

Jacob was in love with Rachel.

Genesis 29:28

Love: a temporary insanity, curable by marriage.

Ambrose Bierce

In the weird world of marital communication, it is often my privilege to ask what Aunt Agony calls "trap door" questions. These are questions that have no right or wrong answers but traps the designated respondent on shaky ground. When the respondent answers the question, doors mysteriously open. Whoosh! Down the respondent goes into the murky waters of "I knew I should have kept my mouth shut!"

The questions cover a variety of subjects. They range from "Do I look fat in this outfit?" to "Do I look younger with my hair up or down?" Or "Do these shoes make my feet look big?" to "Is this dress too tight?" Or "Should I wear the bikini or the one piece on the beach?" to "What does your mother really think about me?"

So, in true form, I asked my husband Stan when did he know that he was in love with me.

"Is this a trick question?" he asked.

"No. There is no right or wrong answer. Just tell me when you knew." I said.

"Is it important?," he asked.

"Yes, of course. I wouldn't have asked you if it weren't important."

"When did I first realize I was in love with you? The same time you realized you were in love with me," he answered with a big grin on his face. As you can see, it takes about thirty-nine years to learn how to navigate "trap door" questions.

Bing and Lorene had been together since high school. He loved her, but he never told her. She loved him and said it often. Basenji was Bing's real name. His name describes an African dog that does not bark.

Bing cannot remember when he first fell in love with Lorene. She can recite chapter and verse about how their relationship developed.

Lorene says that she fell in love with Bing when he first walked in her home room. She fell in love with him when he walked her home on the day when she didn't have enough money to ride the bus. She fell in love with him on the day when he took an extra part-time job to help her get through college. She fell in love with him on the day when he accompanied her to her father's funeral even though her family was against their relationship. Lorene wanted to move in with Bing but he said, "No, let's get married instead." She fell in love all over again.

Bing doesn't even have a clue. Lorene was clear that there were three things Bing did for her: first, he made her laugh; second, he lifted her spirits; and third, he listened to her and let her know that she wasn't always Ms. Right. Mignon McLaughlin writes that a successful marriage requires a couple to fall in love many times—and always with the same person.

Jacob was in love. It all started with a kiss at a well in the middle of a field. And it all happened so fast. As a young poet, Joi-Marie wrote in the movie *Love Jones*, "Like a cool drink down a thirsty throat, you satisfy me. Like a loose string on a crocheted shirt, you unravel me. Love sick, you got me."

Sometimes after having a conversation with someone, a person might say that it seems as though they had known the other person for years. Dr. Harvelle Hendrix in *Getting the Love You Want* calls this the "phenomenon of recognition." When lovers say that it seems as if they have always been together, like Lorene and Bing, it is called the "phenomenon of timelessness."

When lovers say that they cannot live without each other, Dr. Hendrix calls this the "phenomenon of necessity." When couples feel that the other completes who they are as a person, Dr. Hendrix calls this the "phenomenon of reunification."

When Jacob saw Rachel, perhaps he felt the "phenomenon of recognition." Rachel matched the archetype image of his soul mate. He saluted her with a kiss and became overwhelmed with emotions so much so that he wept uncontrollably.

In our 21st century culture, men do not usually cry in public. Unless of course, says Aunt Agony, it is after winning the Final Four college basketball tournament or the Super Bowl game, or hitting the Power Ball lottery.

As cynical as Aunt Agony can be at times, I have seen men weep for joy when they encounter Jesus. Yes, men who would never display emotions in public have stood at the altar of God with tears in their eyes because they had found Jesus or they had finally allowed the spirit of Jesus to enter their hearts!

My husband (don't tell him I said this) was misty eyed when our third child, Joi, in spite of the umbilical cord wrapped around her neck, came into this world. Again, tears flowed when our second born, Vashti Jasmine, successfully made her entrance into the world in spite of being breach. He dappled his eyes when our oldest son, John, hit a snag in the road and almost didn't meet his future.

It was my 200 pound, six foot six inch husband who looked at me with watery eyes on the night of my election and consecration as the first female bishop elected in the African Methodist Episcopal Church. His heart was on the line as much as mine during the four years of campaigning and more than thirty years of ministry. This is where Aunt Agony puts on her "Men Have Feelings Too!" tee shirt.

Men have many ways to express how they feel about those whom they love. Some are romantics and remember anniversaries, send flowers or give meaningful gifts. These are the hand holders, back rubbers and bubble bath aficionados.

There are also men who express themselves in other ways. They work two jobs, pay the bills, buy a house or coach their kid's soccer team. These men would rather show you how much they love you by providing for you rather than saying "I love you" with a tangible gift.

There are those who are wordsmiths. They always know what to say—"My life would be empty without you" or "You've had a hard day, let me massage your feet."

Aunt Agony has only one request, if you are blessed to have a man like that at home, be a sisterfriend and have him cloned for the good of the cause!

There are those who are charmers. They can charm a snake out of its skin and a woman out of a bad mood. It's all good as long as he doesn't charm his way into a place where he shouldn't be. It is also good as long as the person is not slick enough to make a lie sound like the truth or charm their way out of responsibilities such as paying for dinner, washing dishes or paying child support.

There are men who are not as demonstrative as some women would like them to be. They do not mirror poignant platitudes, misty eyes or pained expressions. Since their manner of expression is different than what might be expected or wanted, there is a tendency to believe that these men are incapable of meeting someone else's emotional needs. They are emotionally challenged, and far too trained by their culture and society to suck it up and act like a man.

We do not all march to the same beat. This is when Aunt Agony suggests that you consult your "internal love decoder." Some call it intuition; I call it the Holy Spirit. Put your antennae up so you can pick up unobvious signals that let you know whether the man in your life is into you as much as you are into him. Discern the subtle body behavior to see if, in spite of what it looks and sound like, it is a good deal. Dr. Phil says, "Trust your gut. "

Laban welcomed Jacob into his home. Jacob gave an account of how and why he had come to Syria. He arrived empty handed. There was no caravan of supplies following him. There were no herds of animals to support him or for him to use as barter. There was no mention of sacks of coins to compensate his host. At worse, Jacob was beset by thieves and at best he arrived after being at a place he named Bethel, the house of God. He left home as Jacob and arrived in Syria with a promise from God.

God had a plan. In spite of our need to manipulate our daily events, God works in, through, and around us to achieve God's intended purpose. Jacob left one controversy and arrived to initiate another one. He left as a prodigal son of sorts and arrived with nation potential.

In the midst of humankind's manipulations, God was laying the foundation of a nation. The grace that Jacob received was neither deserved nor earned. Grace showed up like the perennial mint that grew in between the broken cracks in Aunt Agony's back yard. It was also like the dandelions growing through the cracks on the front walkway to our home.

Jacob would not appear on the "most likely to succeed list." God had to do the unexpected.

Laban listened to Jacob's explanation of why a well-endowed man with a promise and a future was sent to relocate with distant relatives. It is reminiscent of what many families did with those who got into trouble or were in danger. They were banished to a family's ancestral home with distant relatives—far from nosey neighbors. It kept them out of harm's way and avoided a public family embarrassment.

Jacob's uncle accepted his explanations about how he had been sent away from his family in the final years of his father's life. There are some scholars who postulate that the original plan was always for Jacob and Esau to find wives in Laban's house. Whether this is fact or theory, Laban welcomes his sister's son into his home.

In the ensuing month, Jacob resided with Laban as a guest. This could be construed as a probationary period, so that Laban could closely observe Jacob. Habits, good and bad, could be discerned. Laban could observe how Jacob responded to family life and even family fights. His reactions would either be pleasing or be the "little foxes that spoil the vine." (2 Solomon 2:15) He could see how Jacob related to and communicated with other family members and household staff. Where do you think he would best fit? In the fields with cattle, goats and sheep or in the fields where he could harvest the soil?

Jacob's interests would surface in conversation. His intellect or lack thereof, would become visible. Laban could have been a cautious parent during this time. After all, the desert grapevine could have spilled the beans about Jacob's disrespect for the local water rights system. Remember, he kissed Rachel and wept loudly. Laban took the time to discern what measure of man Jacob was.

Laban watched Jacob watch Rachel. Imagine Jacob watching Rachel as she went about her daily responsibilities. In the early morning as the women went to draw water for their household needs, Jacob searched for Rachel. Sitting in the common tent, he was patient while Rachel served his meals, always hoping to feel the sudden rush of emotions as she brushed his hand while setting his plate.

Jacob would watch her across a crowded courtyard hoping she would look in his direction. He searched her face for any sign that showed she felt the same about him. He went out of his way to show up, coincidently, at the well to help her draw water for her flocks.

Jacob was melancholy but he never touched Rachel as she took her father's sheep to graze in nearby fields. The smitten kinsman may have just been taking his time to see if she was more than a pretty face. Maybe he wanted to see how she interacted with others. Is Rachel shrewd or a shrew, cautious or careless, cruel or compassionate, greedy or needy? Is this the one or should he look for another. Isn't love grand?

There is, however, another possibility. The thirty day probation period between Jacob's arrival and a job offer from Laban was needed so that Laban could devise his own trap door question. Laban needed time to develop his own manipulative and deceitful plan. He would find a way to use Jacob's carnal desires against him.

Jacob had already demonstrated that he was strong. He was self-motivated and a problem solver. He would take the initiative to circumvent rules to help others.

Another possibility is that in thirty days, Rachel would have her regular menses cycle. The natural menses of a woman was an indication that she was not pregnant. This was a means to protect the family's bloodline. It also indicated that she was old enough to procreate. God had promised that descendents were in the future. The descendents of Adam and Eve were to be fruitful and multiply. Rachel had the equipment and it was imperative that it worked.

Perhaps Jacob's agenda was to see if he had competition. Surely, he wanted to make sure that his tears were not simply a dramatic first response or infatuation.

Aunt Agony reminds us that love comes in many colors. There is the cotton candy pink of infatuation. This color demonstrates a fascination, crazed feelings, or an obsession for someone. The rosy color of puppy love is an "Awwww!" factor. When you are with that special someone, you get the same cute, warm and fuzzy feeling that you might get when you hold an adorable puppy. The problem with this feeling is that puppies grow up and you can grow out of the "awwww!" stage.

In the ruby red of passion, there is the hyperventilating tingling sensation. The lush magenta of lust creates a hungry achy yearning in the pit of the belly. Then there is the true blue of friendship. This denotes genuine care, mutual respect, and loyalty. The apex is the lightening white of agape love or Godly love.

The vivid scarlet of love has always been a challenge. "What is Love?" is a question Shakespeare asks in *Twelfth Night*.

In our struggle to define love, it is often compared with other things. "Water is like love," writes Elie Wiesel. "We only appreciate it in its absence. To the thirsty it stands for happiness; to the slaked, the satisfied, it represents the banality of everyday life." In the Song of Solomon, love is more delightful than wine. (Song of Solomon 2:5)

Love is like a luscious piece of fruit. You don't really know how sweet it is until you bite into it. Love is like the sun. It pretends to die only to return each morning to banish the darkness of the soul.

One night at a Circle of Love session, some women thought love was a feeling; an emotion or a mystical unique bond between two people. Love was being taken care of and taking care of someone else. Love was looking out for one another. Love was showing respect for each other; supporting each other's dreams or being there for someone emotionally and physically.

Aunt Agony says she knows exactly what love is. "It is the crazy something that comes over you and makes you share the remote when "Law and Order" is on—even though your mate might want to watch the game on ESPN. That's love!"

Paul says love is patient and kind. It is neither envious nor boastful. Love is not rude, self-seeking or easily angered. It does not keep a ledger of wrongs. It delights in the good not the evil, rejoicing with the truth. Love always protects trust, hopes and perseveres. Love never fails. Faith and hope rivals love as a prime directive. Love however is the greatest of these. (1 Corinthian 13)

Ask anyone why they love that special someone. They will either give a ready response, a reflective pronouncement or a response disconnected from their personal reality. These are some of the general responses: "I love him because he cares for me." "She helps me." "He makes me feel great." "He provides for me and my children." "She is available to me." He fixes things around the house for me." "He takes me places." "She listens to me." Or simply "because she loves me."

The operative word in those types of responses is "me." They love the other because of what the person does for them. Is this being in love or being in need? The other supplies all my needs; ergo, I need him in my life.

Genuine love cares for the person. I love you because of who you are, not just for what you do for me. My soul connects with the goodness found in your soul. The essence of your integrity speaks to my spirit.

When we express our love for God, is it because of what God has done for us? Does your "I love you, Lord" extend beyond the hand of God that contains every perfect gift? How then do you love God who wants us to return the love? God is a jealous God. God does not want us to deify anything or anyone including spouses, children, Louis Vuitton, Tiffany, Neiman Marcus, a career, an athlete or a platinum American Express card.

Loving the Devine includes seeking the heart of God and having the mind of Christ. It is reaching for the unsearchable riches of Christ that stretch us beyond cycles of bitterness and unforgiveness. It tastes and sees that God is good. It is secure enough to rest on the bosom of the Godhead. The Holy Spirit performs open heart surgery to initiate the flow of agape love to and through us so that we can reflect the infinite character and nature of God.

What is love? If you are still confused, the Bible declares profoundly, God is Love.

Yale University psychologist Robert Sternberg wrote in his book *The Triangle of Love* of a three-pronged approach to love. He concludes that love has three sides: passion, intimacy and commitment. Passion is the physiological side of the triangle. He describes it as the intense physical arousal that is also sensual and sexual. He believes that passion is self-seeking until it is connected to intimacy.

Passion's intensity comes with the glow of a new relationship. The match is struck in Jacob and Rachel styles. The excitement takes the couple to a euphoric high. As a blossom fades and leaves turn in autumn, the intensity of passion fades.

Some researchers conclude that this is the biological side of love. Passion produces natural chemicals in the brain. The brain builds up a tolerance to the chemicals and the intensity diminishes. This is the stage when people think they are no longer in love because they do not feel the same intensity a month, a year or even years later. The color fades and the bloom falls off the stem.

The mistake many couples make is to think the plant is incapable of blooming again. There is a perennial-like quality to longer lasting compassionate love according to T. Miracle, A. Miracle and R. Baumeister in *Human Sexuality: Meeting Your Basic Needs*. The cooling down of passion may be a signal that the developing relationship is transitioning to the next level. Love is not over. It is morphing into the next stage.

Karly thought her husband Ron didn't love her anymore. "He used to call me twice a day just to see what I was doing," she said. "He couldn't keep his hands off me. He held my hand when we went out. He mouthed, 'I love you,' across crowded rooms. He said he was lonely for me during the day and couldn't wait to have X-rated evenings."

She said Ron was working so hard that he forgets to call. He was coming home late. He was constantly missing their regularly scheduled dinners. The little things that he had done to make her feel special, he didn't do anymore.

When Karly confronted Ron, he said his love had not changed. She accused him of seeing someone else. They spent the night amid tears and accusations.

The challenges of making a life together can work to diminish passion's fire. Passion was buried under Ron's workload and Karly wasn't feeling that "special glow" anymore. The patter of little feet late at night into a parent's bedroom can also dampen passion. Perhaps familiarity was setting in; taking the place of the spanking new blossom that was fading.

Miracle and his coauthors concluded that the brain cannot tolerate being pumped up by the sparks of excitement of freshly minted passion. Chemicals called endorphins kick in to calm the mind. The intensity may decrease as passion evolves into compassionate love. This stage of love provides a different pleasure not necessarily a lesser one.

The second side of Sternberg's triangle is intimacy. This is the emotional side of love that blossoms as each person gets to know the other. Intimacy speaks of knowing how the other responds to certain stimuli, what they think about issues, and how they feel about a variety of things.

Couples who have achieved intimacy share and keep secrets. They disclose details of themselves that develops a deep bond of devotion and friendship.

In courtship, everyone is trying to be on their best behavior. The "getting to know you, getting to know all about you" of intimacy goes beyond likes and dislikes. They know the root from which the other springs forth. They trust the other with the truth about themselves. They share things that they may or may not have ever shared with anyone before.

He knows what she looks like without makeup. She knows what he looks like when he needs a shave and a haircut. He knows why she hordes things. She knows why he doesn't know how to pay a bill. He knows why she is a neat freak. She's learned how to put the toilet seat down. He knows why she bristles when her mother calls. She knows why he avoids certain conversations.

They find security in intimacy's honest communication and commitment. There is closeness like the kind that the lover in the Song of Solomon wanted—"Keep me close to yourself like the ring on your finger." (Song of Solomon 8:6)

Stan is my lover, roommate, and my best friend. He didn't become my best friend overnight. We had to walk through some tough experiences together. We learned to lean on each other and laugh everyday. We learned how to give each other space and hold each other close. We both have a hard time getting a good night's sleep when we are apart.

We learned to jettison old arguments, mend fences, share thoughts and say, "I'm sorry." We have learned how to dance in the kitchen to the melodious voice of Luther Vandross after a hectic day, help each other with our dreams as silly or impossible as they may be, spoil each other, tactfully tell each other the truth, celebrate everything, and eat ice cream late at night while huddled under the covers and listening to a Jay Leno monologue.

Stan learned how not to attempt to solve the problems that I share—well, most of the time. I learned to share what was troubling me except when confidentiality issues were involved.

Intimacy takes work. You have to work at it on a regular basis or the relationship will grind to a halt. Many marriages and relationships die a slow death because intimacy has been lost along the way.

Long trips and no maintenance will ruin the engine of a car. Planting a garden without water and weeding will kill the harvest. Exercising without warming up and cooling down can be harmful to your muscles.

Karly and Ron came to realize that their sparks could evolve into a deeper level of intimacy. It required a commitment to be fully present with each other as they pulled back their personal layers to become one flesh in a lifetime of discovery.

Passion is an uncut flower. It withers and dies. Intimacy is a potted plant. Nurture it. Feed it. Give it the proper exposure to sun and soil and it will grow profusely.

The third side of Sternberg's triangle is commitment. It is the willful or cognitive side of love's triangle. Commitment becomes the anchor that holds intimacy and passion steady on the sea of uncertainty. Commitment says you stick around even when trouble starts. It trims the sails and drops the anchor to ride out the storm. It is not capricious but makes an effort to work things out.

Commitment is the richer or poorer, in sickness and in health, from this day forward until death do us part. The 21st century mind-set would probably reword the marriage vows from until death do us part to until we don't feel like it anymore.

The prophet Hosea remained committed to his wife, the harlot. God encouraged him to retrieve her from her lover's bed.

Jacob's passion meter was running high. The Bible says he loved Rachel. In any case, whether it was an audition or a planning period, Jacob may not have been aware that he was being observed and about to match wits with his equal or someone better.

His host finally issues an invitation to earn a living while in residence. He asked the trap door question. What shall I pay you? Remember, the answer to a trap door question either is wrong or gets you in trouble. He asked about the terms of employment and the necessary exchange of goods of services that would be required.

Then, Jacob takes the opportunity to state his love for Laban's youngest daughter, Rachel. He has nothing of substance to offer Laban in exchange for Rachel's hand in marriage. Jacob agrees to work seven years in exchange for Laban's daughter.

In ancient cultures, marriages were often equated with politics, social position and money. In Africa, the Pacific Rim and other parts of the world, families still arrange their offspring's marriage. People did not volunteer to be in an "arranged" marriage. It was not a mutual relationship based on love. A marriage based on love with consenting adults is a relatively new phenomenon in the Western world. Love and romance existed but it wasn't always the impetus for marriage.

Perhaps, the rise of individual rights and the changing roles of women fueled the desire for a relationship based on personal choice rather than by pairings formed by manipulative parents. Hendrix claims that people choose their mates based on their parents' deficiencies. People seek partners who can give them what they did not receive from their parents or caregivers.

Historically, there is also a form of marriage that Hendrix calls a "slave marriage." A wife is purchased by using the community's common means of exchange. The purchase price may be in commodities, cattle or coins. The wife has no rights beyond the upkeep of the home and raising children; after all, she owns no property. The wife is an asset that can be sold.

If Laban was generous enough to pay Jacob $7.00 per hour for an eight hour day, he would earn $56.00 per day. Jacob would earn $392 per week, $1,568 per month, $18,816 per year and $131,712 in seven years.

Jacob loved Rachel. His marriage was based on love and the exchange of goods and services. Seven years is a long time to work for one woman. Jacob evidently thought Rachel was worth it. Love will make you do all kinds of things. It made Jacob become an indentured servant.

Aisha worked at a law firm that specializes in hardship cases. The firm took cases that seemed impossible to win and provided pro bono services for those who could not afford legal services.

Jareal's mother came into Aisha's office pleading for assistance. As any concerned parent would implore, her son was innocent. He had been partying at a strip joint with a group of friends. On the way home, he ran a stoplight and the police stopped his car.

A search of the car found drugs, money and guns. It was Jareal's car but he said he didn't know where the stuff came from. No one knew who put it in the car. Everyone pleaded ignorance. They claimed that somebody else must have placed the items in the car while they were in the club.

He, however, was convicted based on the testimony of his companions. They said Jareal left them for at least an hour while they enjoyed lap dances. According to Jareal's companions, it was enough time to make a deal and hide the drugs, money and guns in the car.

Jareal's mother wanted a new trial. She believed her son was set up and, more importantly, the court-ordered attorney didn't help.

Aisha set up an interview with Jareal at the prison. Upon first impression, he didn't seem like a drug dealer. He was college educated. And prior to his arrest, he had a promising career with a utility company. How could he become involved with drugs in the first place? Jareal was a victim, not a perpetrator.

Aisha made frequent visits to prison in an effort to get the details of the events. In the beginning, her sessions were strictly business. Later, however, they became rather personal. Every day, Aisha and Jareal talked. She longed to sit across from him at the interview table so that he could look at her lustfully. He had "McDreamy" eyes that swept over her entire body. His voice was silky and he skillfully used it when he would say her name, and say things to her that no other man would dare to imagine.

He quoted poetry like Doughtry Long's "Ginger Bread Mama": "I love you ginger bread mama, ginger bread mama, all sweet and brown; love you more than tired boys love collard greens and candied yams, more than new watermelons do the sun. . . ."

Aisha declared she was in love.

Aisha's hard work paid off. She received a change of venue. The retrial would be held in a different municipality and away from the glaring attention of the media. No one knew, however, that Aisha and Jareal had planned his escape. She studied the security system and routines like she studied for her bar exam.

Aisha would help the man she loved to escape. They would live happily ever after. Happily ever after has ruined more than one marriage. Why? Because it sets up unrealistic expectations. Some people believe that once you are married, everything will be all right. Your problems will be over and you will forever sail on the seas of love. This assumption, however, doesn't take in account high winds, water currents or choppy waves.

You probably already know Aisha's and Jareal's ending. The plan failed and they are both serving time.

A chaplain friend of mine told me this story. The chaplain asked Aisha why she did it, why Aisha would throw away a promising career in law. Aisha responded that love made her do it.

Love blindsided her. Jareal sucked her into his world. She was stuck on stupid. She was stuck in a moment and couldn't get out.

Erwin McManus writes that moments are as numerous as there are stars in the sky and sand at the seashore. Any one could prove to be the most significant moment in your life. He says that only a handful of moments are moments where the choices you make determine the course and momentum of your life.

Some moments are overwhelming. When Halle Berry received her Oscar for best actress in a leading role, she was overwhelmed by the moment. She began her remarks by saying: "This moment is so much bigger than me."

These are the moments that intersect with the past and the future. Her moment in the sun was validation of years of sacrifice and hard work—work started by others who built the pathway that she walked to receive her Oscar. Likewise, this moment in the sun would be the bridge over which others would walk.

Aisha's moment was an open door to tragedy. Many years ago there was a song that said "stuck in a moment you can't get out of." It was a moment that would not let go. It was a moment in Aisha's history that would forever dominate her present and future.

Aisha confused her desire to help with her need to be loved, to be cherished and to be special in someone else's eyes. Jareal rang her bell. She was in a place in life where she was willing to throw caution and common sense to the wind—all for a chance to live with a "bad boy."

Brea didn't know that the love of her life was a switch hitter. He loved woman and men with equal tenacity. He rolled regularly between her bed and that of a man named Carroll.

Brea loved Sonny. They lived near a lake thirty minutes from work and home. Sonny spent most of his free time fishing from their houseboat or traveling for his job.

Brea never went to the houseboat because she was afraid of water. She never went on the road with her husband because she was afraid to fly. Her fears and phobias kept her from spending any play time with the man she loved.

On New Year's Eve, she made a commitment to address her issues. She secretly sought counseling for her fears. She was tired of being afraid. She was tired of the nickname her husband gave her, "Nervous Nellie."

One weekend, she decided to surprise Sonny on the house boat. She fixed his lunch, as usual. She packed his bag, as usual. She kissed him goodbye at the door, as usual.

Brea gave him a head start then followed him to the lake. On the previous evening, she had secretly packed her overnight bag and loaded it with goodies—a new negligee to drive him crazy and a few bedroom toys suggested by a girlfriend.

She arrived at the houseboat. She was excited. The anticipation was driving her insane. She knew they were going to spend an intimate weekend on their houseboat. Sonny would forget all about fishing.

When Brea slipped into the houseboat, she hoped to surprise him. Sonny, however, wasn't on deck getting his rods and reels ready. He was already in the bedroom.

Sonny was in bed with a man. She stood in the door, stunned, and unable to move. Carroll quickly got up and hid in the bathroom. Brea doesn't remember when she started to scream or throw things. She unleashed venom on Sonny. It was over. Sonny was over. There was no need for him to come home. She would send his stuff to wherever he was going to live.

In the aftermath, Brea figured it was her fault. She told herself that she should have tried harder to please her husband. She should have started counseling sooner so that he could never label her as "Nervous Nellie." She should have gone with him to the houseboat and on trips. She developed a long list of "oughts" and "shoulds."

Brea didn't realize that Sonny had been in a homosexual relationship before they got married. It continued even after their wedding vows. Now, Brea trusts no one—and especially their sexuality. It will be a long time before she trusts again.

Brea was blinded by love. Her love was exploited by someone who wanted the best of two worlds. She was stuck on stupid not because she trusted him but because she blamed herself for someone else's choice.

Jacob loved Rachel and was willing to indenture himself for seven years.

In our 21st century culture, it is frightening to know that some of us take more time to select a car than we do to select a mate. We spend months reading advertisements for the best deals. We go on the internet to review statistical data that shows us miles per gallon, warranty coverages and resale values.

We will go from lot to lot looking for the right color and perfect interior. We will dicker for hours with sales personnel trying to negotiate an affordable price. We will spend time and energy to select the right hairdresser, manicurist, pharmacist, accountant, insurance agent and doctor.

When it comes to spouses, lovers, good friends or the people with whom we share our lives, we exhibit less tenacity. We spend more time choosing church membership and which translation of the Bible to study than we do on those who will occupy the secret chambers of our lives. We pin our hopes, dreams and expectations on a chemical response or a gut reaction.

Aisha forgot who she was when she went to interview Jareal. She got sidetracked with a unhealthy desire to fulfill a little girl's fantasy. Brea liked what she saw on the outside but didn't really want to believe the clues Sonny was leaving behind. He ridiculed her fearful nature rather than help her to work through them. He manipulated her fears to make room for his extracurricular activities—just like Laban was going to manipulate Jacob's feelings for Rachel.

When I asked the women in the Circle of Love what it felt like to be in love, the descriptions ranged from "It sucks" to "It's sensational." One woman was not quite sure whether love was a hormonal surge or the result of a deluded mind.

Everyone wants to be loved and cherished. We want those moments that come when someone volunteers to share their lives with us and we uncontrollably want to share our lives with them. It is crazy.

Sometimes it knocks us down or sneaks up on us, tempting us to move from selfish to common agendas. All the things we said we wouldn't do, we do. We grin like fools, talk like idiots, and text message stuff that is embarrassing, all in the name of love.

I remember the moment, the minute, day, and hour when love rearranged my well planned agenda. Stan and Bing may be clueless about when love happened but what is important is that love happened.

What really mattered is that Stan and I stuck like glue—even when we could not define our evolution and our ebb and flow of triangular love. It doesn't matter whether it takes less than a year or many years to know that you are in love. What's important is that you realize that what you were looking for, you already had in your possession.

S.M.A.R.T. MOVES

(Spiritual Motivation for Action and Real Transformation)

Talking Points

1. What is your definition of love?

2. Describe how you and your partner learned how to become intimate.

3. Have you ever done something stupid in the name of love?

4. Have you ever been stuck in a moment that you couldn't get out of?

5. Have you ever dated uptown or downtown? Dating uptown is when you connect with a person who makes you look good or has a higher standard of living than you. Downtown dating is when you connect to gangster elements. They are those who live down, dirty or dangerously.

The Word in Prayer

In case you haven't figured this out, this is my silent prayer said out loud.

> To bring me a man that was fitting in only a me-kinda-way.
> That understood my imperfections but never judged me for them.
> That didn't always understand my family, my circumstance, my future, or my past but understood that it was okay for me to mess up, to be human, to err and still have the capability to love me.
> And as I finally look into your eyes, by simply closing mine, I'm reminded that I
> Knew you before . . . before I was me and you were you . . . I knew you . . . and I thank
> God for you . . . this is my poem for us, my hope for us, this is my prayer for us.
> Amen." —Joi-Marie.

The Word of God

"Give thanks to the Lord, for he is good; his love endures forever." (Psalm 118:1)

Foreplay

Mornings can be hectic. Just getting out of the house on time takes major effort. This morning surprise your spouse or significant other by suggesting to save time the two of you should shower together. Bring body wash to rub his back and he yours.

Pillow Talk

Share one thing briefly that is important to you. Say "Good night" and kiss your special someone like you mean it!

Kiss and Tell

When you leave a note, any note anywhere, remember to tell your special someone that you are still in love with them.

Kiss and Make Up

Emotional intimacy is not easy for some people. Disclosure is like being fully clothed and jumping into the deep end of the pool. Some people may believe that they are headed straight to the bottom. If your partner is a morning person, that may be a good time to share from your heart. If he is a night owl, stay up and share. Find the time that works for both of you.

Marital Madness

Saying "I love you" with strings attached.

Singularity

Saying "I love you" with strings attached.

F O U R

P I C K I N G   U P   T H E   P I E C E S

What is this you have done to me?
Genesis 29:25

Do not fret because of evil men. . . .
Delight yourself in the Lord and he will give you
the desires of your heart.
Psalm 37:1–7

There is an ancient myth about a man named Tantalus. Tantalus was a man condemned to live eternally in water that he couldn't drink and see beautiful boughs of fruit that he could not eat. The abundance of fruit was always beyond his reach.

Jacob had a Tantalus experience. Rachel was his beloved but he could not have her as his wife. He lived in Laban's camp with a woman he loved but could not touch. He wanted her but could not have her for seven years. Being content to see her each day, he labored day and night for the right to marry her. His love was unrequited. He desired Rachel and only Rachel.

What is a desire? Plato says that desire is a fundamental power of the soul. He describes it in his *Symposium* as a ladder between heaven and earth. Jacob already dreamed of a ladder between heaven and earth.

In *Phaedrus*, Plato describes desire as something that enables the soul to feast on truth. Augustine describes desire as a weight that draws our hearts more irresistibly than gravity draws the body. Desire, therefore, becomes stronger than will power.

Another writer says that desire is like a burning light that may diminish but cannot be completely extinguished. Desire is the "beautiful scathing brand" that reminds us who we are and to whom we belong.

The Psalmist describes desire as a hart, or deer, who pants for water—this is our desire for God. The Psalmist also indicates that God grants us the desires of our hearts.

Oftentimes, we believe that the desire of our heart is something that can be possessed, owned or obtained. We live in a consumer driven culture. No matter what we own or how much we have, there is always something newer and better than what we can afford. We are surrounded by images and advertisements that promise us beauty, peace, love, security, happy families, lovely homes, sex, pride, higher self esteem, and longevity.

We are offered an unending variety of material and nonmaterial goods, yet still the heart hungers for more. This desire delights in things but is never satisfied.

According to John Eldredge in his book *The Journey of Desire*, desire cannot be satisfied with any finite thing or any number of finite things. Therefore, the heart hungers for something more than a new shiny pair of skates.

Desire thirsts for more than what the world has to offer, writes Eldredge. It doesn't reject the goods of the world but it recognizes that it doesn't hold the key to our happiness. Desire goes deeper, deepening the capacity for joy. Desire pulls us out of ourselves. It can also pull us towards who we were created to be.

Desire can be like fire shut up in our bones. It can be a grain of sand irritating an oyster that is mysteriously transformed into a pearl. It can be money forgotten in a pocket that is found years later—and just when it is needed.

Eldredge writes that desire holds open the door of possibility. It is resourceful and tells us what it sees. Desire teases, taunts, and tantalizes us until we are willing to forget everything to find its joy.

Desire transformed the years into days for Jacob. He was paying a higher price because he was not in a position to negotiate. Jacob paid Laban seven years of his labor to marry his beloved. This, according to the Nuzi texts, was substantially larger than the typical price for a bride—30 to 40 shekels of silver.

Jacob said to Laban, "Give me my wife. My time is completed, and I want to lie with her." So Laban bought together all the people of the place and gave a feast. (Genesis 29:21–22)

Weddings in this ancient culture were a consummation of a contract between two families. It was a week of festivities that were large social gatherings that included a ritual meal and a procession to the designated new home. Matthew 25:1–13 gives a portrait of the wedding feast. The bridegroom would bring the bride from her parent's home. Accompanied with music and singing, the bridegroom would then be surrounded by his friends. He would lead the procession through the streets of the town or area to the bride's home. With their lamps lit and burning, friends along the route would be ready to join the procession.

The bride would be heavily veiled in embroidered attired. She may be adorned with jewels. Her attendants would accompany her in the procession.

Upon arriving at the home, the Song of Solomon indicates, the bridal couple would sit under a canopy. (Song of Solomon 2:4) Food and wine is enjoyed by everyone as people filled the tent or home. (John 2:1–11) The wedding would last a week. In some cases, the bridal couple and guests wore their festive garments the entire time.

The father of the bride would escort his daughter to the wedding chamber or tent. You can picture Jacob as a very happy man. For years, he had looked forward to this feast. Now, he would consummate his love for Rachel.

It may have been Rachel's wedding gown but it was Leah under the veil. It was Leah who was led into the wedding tent. It was Leah's hand Jacob held. It was Leah who surrendered her virginity. It was Leah's blood on the sheets that her father would use to prove her purity if later questioned.

It was Leah's body that Jacob stroked in darkness. Like a gazelle in a hunter's hand, she had no desire to free herself. She offered herself to Jacob so that he could satisfy himself.

Could it be that Leah desired Jacob all along? In one night, she could wipe away the memory of a seven year old kiss at the well. Jacob may have wept at the well but she would have him coming back for more!

Leah usurped her sister's position just like Jacob took Esau's place. Instead of Rachel, Leah laid in her sister's place.

Greg was on Angie's arm when they walked into the banquet room. Her girlfriends were wondering about her new boyfriend. She was officially titled "girlfriend" and they were exclusively dating each other.

Deidre recognized him from her college days. During the evening, she didn't indicate to Angie that she and Greg had a history together.

Later that night, she called him to reignite old times. One thing led to another and they rekindled their relationship. Angie suspected what was going on but refused to confront Greg about his backdoor relationship with Deidre.

She believed if she gave him what Deidre was giving him, then he would choose to stay with her. Greg enjoyed the fruits of his labors.

Dr. Laura Schlessinger writes that sexual acts that are not supportive of your being and soul are stupid sex. Using sexual behavior to keep exclusivity outside of a covenant relationship is also stupid. Thinking sex will keep a man or lead him to the altar is in the same stupidity category as having unprotected sex.

In her book *Ten Stupid Things Men Do to Mess Up Their Lives*, Dr. Laura indicates that having sex with the sister or best friend of a past partner, basing a relationship on sex, and having sex without commitment, compassion or love is a recipe for ruin. She says it is not just having a little fun on the side. Something negative always happens spiritually, emotionally, medically, socially, legally, financially and embarrassingly.

Angie and Deidre were no longer friends. Their circle of companions was split on the issue of who was in the wrong. And almost at the same time, both women became pregnant. Greg had moved on to other fertile fields. He was engaged to be married—neither to Angie or Deidre —and wanted his past to stay in the past.

With great resentment, he paid the medical bills, thinking that *they* should have been more careful. He also agreed to child support but wanted nothing to do with the by-product of his sexual activities. Something "bad" happens. The absence of a father creates children who will have a hole in their heart—a hole where the father should be, says radio's Dr. Laura.

Leah is now waiting for the dawn to arrive. She was waiting for the light to flood into the marriage tent. Waiting, but not knowing that the few hours of darkness that had past may have been her happiest moments.

She held her hopes tightly. Hope is like a kite flying at the end of a string. In an instant, the kite rises with the wind. It glistens in the sun and becomes visible for the world to see. People stop to stare at the kite, as it takes advantage of every up draft. They remember when they had the time to fly their kite. They also remember when their hopes soared to the sky.

Hope dangles at the end of the string seemingly at the mercy of unpredictable winds. It is fragile enough to be tossed in the changing currents yet strong enough to handle the uncertainty of the "sometimes up and sometimes down."

The skill of the kite flyer can keep the kite in the air. The right pull of the strings and slight twists of the wrist, can keep the kite from plummeting to the earth. Sometimes, in spite of the best efforts of the kite flier, it falls to the ground in shreds. Hope fails.

Hope can remain assigned to the ground or the kite flier can pick up the pieces and try again. Hope is not diminished by unfavorable winds. Its strength comes not from the skill of the kite flyer but from the power of the Divine Kite Maker. Those who hope in the Lord shall find renewed strength to fly their kites again! "But those who hope in the Lord will renew their strength. . . ." (Isaiah 40: 31)

Leah's illusion of love fades with the rising of the sun. All along, she hoped that Jacob knew that it was really her and not Rachel. She wanted everything to be all right. Surely Jacob had recognized her figure under her wedding garment.

"It is going to be all right," she told herself, as she waited for the darkness to fade and the first rays of light to reveal her face under the veil. She was hoping against hope that the kisses, sexual interludes and intimacy were so good that Jacob would forget about Rachel. He would love her after all.

Disillusionment unraveled her hopes. In the clear morning, after the effects of wine had faded, Jacob discovers that it is Rachel's sister Leah in his bridal bed. He had wanted and worked for Rachel, not the older sister who the texts described as having weak eyes.

"What have you done to me?" declares Jacob to Laban. Laban now informs him of the custom practiced in the Near East—that of the oldest daughter marrying first. Jacob who had manipulated his father and brother to obtain a blessing that didn't belong to him had now been duped!

He tasted the bitter water of betrayal. He was forced to drink deeply as Laban turned the tables on the trickster. It was a betrayal with benefits.

Jacob had lived with this family for seven years. It would seem as if he should have been able to distinguish between the two sisters. Leah, whose name means gazelle or wild cow, isn't described as being unseemly. Her eyes were just weak. It could have been that her eyes were a different color or gave the appearance of vulnerability. Rachel, whose name means "ewe," may have had an upper hand because she was described as lovely in form and beautiful.

In some cases, the bridal veil was removed and placed on the shoulder of the groom. In other cases, the veil remained intact until the following morning. It is perhaps a combination of too much wine and a thick veil that kept Jacob in the dark about the true identity of the one who occupied his bed.

To uphold the contract, Laban suggested that Jacob complete Leah's bride week to avoid a public embarrassment of Leah and her family. Laban would then give him Rachel to wed in exchange for another seven years labor.

Jacob agreed. He spent the rest of the week in the tent with Leah.

Jacob didn't want her. But he took her anyhow. Leah kept him busy.

According to Aunt Agony, one of the worse feelings a woman could have is to wake up in the morning to find out that she has been used. She's been treated like a garment that had been worn and tossed aside and returned to the place of purchase for a store credit.

Jordan began crying the moment the wedding ceremony was over. She could not stop crying. Everyone thought they were tears of joy. She cried through the rituals of cutting the cake, tossing her bouquet, and giving up her garter. She dabbed her eyes with every toast of champagne.

In the limo ride to the airport where they would board a plane to enjoy their honeymoon in Cancun, she told Shawn why she couldn't stop crying. On the eve of their wedding, Shawn's best friend Charles had told her that Shawn had only married her to get back at his parents. They had wanted him to marry someone who had a comparable social standing, and Jordan didn't come from the appropriate lineage or social standing.

This act of rebellion would let them know that he was in charge of his life. What hurt the most was that Shawn wasn't in love with her. She was just a pawn in his plot to have his own way and to control his trust fund. Charles said that Shawn had no intentions, of being married forever. He would stick it out until Jordan was no longer entertaining.

Jordan also cried because she had decided to marry Shawn anyway. She thought that a ring and ceremony would change things. When she looked into his eyes as they said their vows, she knew what the best friend had said was true.

She had been a tool. She was a thing. She was an instrument that had been used to manipulate his plan.

Moreover, Jordan cried because she allowed herself to be used. She willingly walked down the aisle and lied.

Dr. Robin L. Smith writes in *Lies at the Altar* that sometimes it is easier to settle for fantasy than face the truth. She says ask yourself: Do you live in dread that your partner will find out about the real you? Do you present yourself fully and honestly? She says a lie says it is better to have anything than to be alone. Smith says, truthfully, it is better to be alone and free than controlled together.

Another question to ask yourself is about your partner's behavior and attitudes. Does he inspire you or does he drain your spirit, making your stomach turn? Smith says it is a lie to believe that marriage will magically change people, that they will be changed for the better. Smith's truth statement is that the person at the altar in the afternoon will be the same person at the breakfast table in the morning.

Jordan and Shawn had married for the wrong reasons. One married as an act of rebellion. The other believed that everything bad would disappear and everything good would appear.

Leah was a pawn in her father's scheme. She was a means to obtain free labor from Jacob. Like Jordan, Leah waited and hoped that everything bad would disappear and everything good would appear.

Dr. Jeremiah Wright, in his sermon "Jacob's Naughty Nature," wanted to know what Jacob had to say for himself. Jacob wanted one woman and got tricked into marrying another. Jacob's situation is like that of many people who are tricked into shotgun marriage arrangements—even in a day when birth control pills, patches, foam, rings and adoptions are available. Unlike Jacob, whose father-in-law swapped housewives, today many men are tricked with claims of pregnancies—pregnancies that mysteriously disappear after the ceremony.

Dr. Wright said that Jacob was married to one but loved another. Many men have been down that street or may still be living on it. He said that Leah and Rachel must have been built alike and kissed alike for Jacob to not notice anything. In the end, he may have loved one but preferred to procreate through the other.

According to Dr. Wright, Jacob's silence to his question of Laban is answered by the eloquence of Paul in Romans 7:4–25. He said Jacob is simply naughty by nature. He spent his life concerned more about things than people. He's plotted and planned schemed and scammed.

Jacob's human nature served the law of sin. The good that I would do, I do not do. The sin that I do not want to do, I do. (Romans 7:18) Jacob was held hostage by his own habits. He was a prisoner of his habits and like Greg, Jacob enjoyed the fruits of his labors with Leah and Rachel.

Aunt Agony says there is nothing worse than a DOA relationship—one that is "dead on arrival." Leah was handed over to Jacob like a commodity. She had a future with a man where there was no chance of love. Rachel had to share her future husband with her sister. Any visions of exclusive wedded bliss had evaporated.

Rachel had to help celebrate the new couple. She helped to prepare the food and wine for what should have been her wedding feast. She had to listen to the sounds of lovemaking coming from the wedding tent— Jacob satisfying himself with a woman he did not love.

They were linked into an unexpected future. Each woman played her part in their father's wrangling deception.

Who is going to help them pick up the pieces?

In *The Pebble and the Avalanche*, Moshe Yudkowsy writes that an avalanche can begin with a tiny pebble. It dislodges more pebbles until larger rocks start to move, thus triggering a landslide. An avalanche releases incredible energy and in spite of its massive power, it finally comes to a stop. When all is said and done, you will still have most of the pieces you started with. Jacob and Rachel and Leah just had a major avalanche.

Have you had any avalanches lately? It is a part of the human condition that sometimes pebbles will dislodge and find themselves at the bottom of your hill. How we respond to our avalanche is often determined by how we think of them, how we manage our mind.

A negative thinking person has the flair to define the problem while a positive thinking person has a gift to point out the solution. The pessimist can tell you when the pebbles will fall, the rate of speed of each stone, the exact location and time of the disaster, how long it took for the mountain to move to the bottom of the hill, and why the rescue effort failed.

On the other hand, the optimist looks at the pile of rubble and says, "At the top of the hill, there still remain most of the pebbles that I started with."

The pebbles are not gone. They are just at the bottom of the hill. They can be used to build walls, homes, communities, and countries. They are just in a different location. You can still use them to put your life back together again.

The pessimist says, "All hope is gone," but the optimist says, "Hope thou in God." The pessimist sees it as a threat while the optimist sees it as a challenge. The pessimist sees defeat and the optimist sees victory waiting in the wings. The pessimist "awfulizes" while the optimist strategizes.

Psychologist Albert Ellis writes that "awfulizing" is when you mentally magnify a problem until it has the greatest dire consequences. It is making a mountain out of a molehill; it is making the most out of obsessive worrying—exaggerating the situation until you become incapacitated.

Truthfully, in these uncertain days, is it is easy to "awfulize" situations. Daily, our societal landscape reminds us that it is a jungle out there. Daily, we face media reports of human depravity, crime, and violence.

Isn't it awful that James Brown died on Christmas morning, that Coretta Scott King died, that Saddam Hussein's execution was broadcast on the Internet, that George W. Bush started a war we can't finish, that someone was shot and killed over an Xbox 360, that the price of gasoline has risen to an all-time high, and that prices for everything have risen. Isn't it awful! We do live in a wilderness.

If we are not careful, our conversation can easily be affected by all the negatives that we see and hear around us. We will become like the pessimist if we only talk about the wilderness.

Is it really God's desire for us to become overly consumed by wilderness conversation when the prophet Isaiah tells us that God will make a way through the wilderness? (Isaiah 43:18–19)

The prophetic voice of Isaiah is directed to God's people who are exiled in Babylon. This was their avalanche: the city of God—Jerusalem—was destroyed, reduced to rubble, gates burned and the temple ransacked. Its leadership was deposed and in confusion. The best and brightest were taken captive; the intellectual and artistic capital oppressed. They experienced a sense of hopelessness. The Psalmist declared that they could not sing the lord's song in a strange land. So they hung their harps on the willow tree to sing no more.

The people of God were "awfulizing." When you "awfulize," according to Martin Seligman, author of *Learned Optimism,* we take stuff personally and blame ourselves. We see the avalanche as pervasive. This is just another thing that proves our incompetence. Finally, he notes, we think that the problem is permanent.

Seligman suggests, instead of feeling helpless, look at the avalanche as a challenge. Be empowered and control what you can control. Be committed to the bigger picture—look beyond the event.

God uses Jacob to build the Israelite nation. His children, borne to four women, are the foundation for the twelve tribes of Israel. Joseph, Rachel's son, saves the family from starvation during a famine. As he concluded at the end of his own enslaved avalanche, what others meant for evil God meant for good. (Genesis 50:20)

The prophet speaks believing they had already received double punishment. In the prophet's mind—and God's, notes one scholar—the people had suffered more than enough. Their season of suffering was coming to an end.

Isaiah reminds them of when God brought their foreparents out of the land of Egypt. A picture of power is painted on the canvas of their "awfulizing" minds to remind them that God has the power over nature and nations.

The sermon builds as he tells them that God was able to make a way through the sea and God is able to do it again—a way through the sea to freedom.

Suddenly, God says forget the former things. Don't "awfulize." After such a buildup God says forget. See, says the Lord, I am doing a new thing. Do you not perceive it? I am making a way in the desert—it is time for a highway to be built so that the exiles will have a way out of their suffering.

In other words, this time, don't expect God to bring deliverance in exactly the same way. Do not hold God to a set formula to solve problems.

You can just imagine it. The people probably thought that God would again send a deliverer just like Moses to part the Red Sea. They probably thought that God would send another Joshua so that they could once again cross the Jordan River on dry land. They probably looked around to see whom God would choose to lead them across the Euphrates River.

Wait, God says, "I am going to do a new thing." What God did last year might not be what God will do this year. Don't hold God to a pattern, a formula, five steps to success, seven steps to prosperity, four steps to the increase, three steps to overflow, twelve steps to the next level, or ten steps to a perfect marriage. Look for God to do a new thing.

What was the new thing that God did for the Israelites that can help us see what new thing God can do for us today?

God broke into their wilderness experience with good news. God broke in with a word of encouragement. I am going to do a new thing—can you sense its coming?

Instead of "awfulizing," live with the expectation that God can break into our lives in a new way. Can you feel it? Breaking through and creating a new path through the wilderness might lead you on the road to something new. Get through and get to something new.

God broke into the lives of the Israelites with good news. God broke up what held them down. The exiles lived under Babylonian rule but the word indicates that a part of the new thing is that God will use someone else to break up the oppression.

God did use King Cyrus of Persia to defeat the Babylonians in 538 B.C.E. One year later, they returned to their homeland. In order to get them out of bondage, God had to break up the old regime, the old order of things. God rearrange the oppressor's furniture. God broke in and broke up the enemy's camp.

God has the power to break up systems that can hold you down and keep you from moving forward. Break up the haters' club, the liars' club, the conspiracy of the devil to rob you of your sanity and peace of mind, and the enemy's plan to steal your joy and your job. Break up some stuff. Defeat your enemies. Break up the camp and by the end of the year, you will get out and get through.

God broke in and broke up the pattern of failure. God made a way through the wilderness and one year later the Israelites were singing God's song in their homeland.

God broke into their lives with good news. God broke up what was holding them down. God broke them out.

Just as God had promised, God delivered. Their prayers were answered, lands restored. They were on their way somewhere.

As God has done for the Israelites, God can do the same for you. I loved the movie *Dreamgirls*. What I loved about the movie was the music, the intrigue, the rags-to-riches story, the clothes, the wolves in sheep clothing, how the bad guys got what was coming to them, and how Jennifer Hudson's character "Effie White" got what she deserved.

I loved how Beyonce's character finally developed a backbone and broke out of a manipulative relationship. *Dreamgirls* was about each singer's breakout moment. Simon from television's *American Idol* allegedly apologized to Jennifer Hudson because he had told her that she would never make it in show business.

There are many prognosticators who will say you can't make it. There are armchair quarterbacks who will second guess your plays. There are your regular girlfriends' predictions about your stuff. There are those who say you will not recover from your relationship setbacks or believe that your life isn't going anywhere.

You will be trapped in a loveless marriage like Leah. You will end up sharing your man with another sister like Rachel. An avalanche will bury you deep in debt or with unexpected responsibilities. New pebbles are falling down your mountain everyday.

Spend time with God by working on a supernatural solution to your problems. Talk more about the new roads and new possibilities. God made a new road for the Hebrews. God has the power to make a new road for you.

This may be your breakout year. Pick up the pieces. You still have most of what you started with. It may be in a different location but you can still use it to put your life back together.

God broke Joseph out of the pit and the prison; the Israelites broke out of Egypt; the three Hebrew boys broke out of the fiery furnace; Daniel broke out of the den of lions; Paul and Silas broke out of jail; and Jesus broke out the tomb with all power in his hand, breaking up sin, death and hell.

This is a breakout year: break out of the law of sin; break out of bad habits; break out of unproductive activities; break out of debt; break out of negative thoughts; break out of negative relationships; break out from being a pessimist to an optimist; break out of poisonous habits; break into a new career, a new ministry, a new business, a school to get a degree, or a new relationship. God is going to forge a new path through your wilderness.

Aunt Agony says she feels like busting loose!

S.M.A.R.T. MOVES
(Spiritual Motivation for Action and Real Transformation)

Talking Points

1. How do you respond to those who see you as a thing to use rather than a person?

2. Have you ever been in a relationship where you willingly "shared" someone with the hope they would choose you?

3. Share some of the things that you "awfulize" about.

4. What are some of the myths you believe about relationships, such as anything is better than being alone?

5. Are you a slave to habits that are not good for you?

6. What does God's Word say about human sexuality?

7. When should a friend speak up when she knows something is detrimental to a relationship?

The Word of Prayer

Break into my life today to help me do the things that are helpful not harmful or self-defeating. Break up any patterns of negative behavior. Break me into a new life where you will help me make wise choices for my life and others. In Jesus' name. Amen.

The Word of God

"Forget the former things; do not dwell on the past. See I am doing a new thing! Now it springs up; do you not perceive it? I am making a way in the desert and streams in the wasteland." (Isaiah 43:18–19)

Foreplay

Today, before you go your separate ways, make a deposit into your partner's or spouse's life by saying one thing you appreciate about him.

Pillow Talk

Make another deposit by saying something nice before you go to sleep. Something like, "I missed you." By all means, be creative.

Kiss and Tell

Kiss your man like you mean it and tell him that "friends don't let friends treat each other like inanimate objects."

Kiss and Make Up

Spend time together in prayer, allowing the healing presence of God to tend to the wounds caused by crushed hopes.

Marital Madness

Do not discuss former boyfriends or expect your partner to be friends with them. Do not compare your partner with any past lovers. Do not make them pay for someone else's manipulations of your life.

Singularity

If you have been around the block a few times, most men don't want to know your journey or with whom you journeyed. You have gone around in circles long enough.

Aunt Agony reminds you that most men want to marry Clare Huxtable while dating Lil' Kim.

FIVE

TRUTH OR CONSEQUENCES

He finished the week with Leah,
and then Laban gave his daughter Rachel
to be his wife.

Genesis 29:28

A working marital relationship is built on trust.

Terry Hargrave, Ph.D.

I n my favorite Roland Park café, Aunt Agony sat down at my table by the window. Looking around to make sure no one was watching, she took off her shoes while gulping down what could have been her 100th cup of coffee.

I diligently destroyed a chicken Caesar salad and sweet potato fries and sipped on my green tea. I was having a late lunch on a Friday afternoon. A late lunch meant I was preparing to pick up the kids from school.

A young woman swept into the café wearing what Aunt Agony called a "pert professional" suit in a Tiffany turquoise color. "Pert professional" is a business suit with a lot of added frills and fluff on the sleeve, collar or hem. And it generally is in a color other than ordinary business blue, black or gray.

The woman who looked thirty-something was drop-dead gorgeous. She had endless legs, a petite waist and red hair that framed her pixie-like face. The two lingering male diners drooled. The other remaining female diners appeared to pay attention to their conversation but out of the corner of their eye, they caught every detail of this young intruder.

In the nearly empty café, she plopped down at the counter. Aunt Agony was off the clock but she rose to see if the new arrival wanted something to eat.

She mumbled something about a cup of coffee and two chocolate chip cookies. The way her slim figure fidgeted on the stool, she looked as if she could handle a dozen chocolate chip cookies with ease.

On the outside, this woman looked as if she was on top of the world. Looks are deceiving. Friends might look like friends but in reality, they could be your enemies. Calm looks calm except when it is right before a storm. A dog can look friendly until it bites, a snake can look harmless until its venomous bite poisons you, a road can appear clear until a sharp turn becomes deadly, and things can often look right until you scratch beneath the surface.

When she just sat there after her food was served, Aunt Agony moved in like an old stealth bomber. She may be out of date but she is always on target.

"Had a rough day?" Aunt Agony inquired. "Had a rough year," the woman responded.

Aunt Agony was about to get comfy so that she could listen to the wayfaring stranger's story but the woman abruptly turned her back to the spandex clad grandmother. Agony returned to my table to retrieve her coffee and her shoes.

The woman's cell phone rang. She began to talk like a lot of people talk on their cell phones in public—just loud enough for everyone to hear and not caring if anyone was listening.

"God answers prayer," whispered Aunt Agony.

Just as much as I was determined not to listen to the woman's conversation, Aunt Agony was equally determined to hear every single word. "I got what I wanted. The ring, the man, the promotion and the raise," said the woman. "But I am not happy. What's wrong with me? I should be happy."

I knew that Aunt Agony would have a new friend and a new café regular. In the coming weeks, Aunt Agony introduced me to Amanda. I invited her to the Circle of Love.

In the Circle, I learned that Amanda was use to getting what she wanted by using what Aunt Agony calls her "feminine wiles." Amanda believed that if people could choose between a show horse who works and a work horse with no show, they would chose the show horse.

Amanda had perfected the art of subtle seduction. She carefully chose her perfume—not too strong but just enough to leave an aromatic memory. She picked out her wardrobe to accentuate her assets. She practiced her walk—a walk that was seductive and suggestive.

Amanda knew how to make an entrance. When she walked into a room, any room be it board room or bathroom, her presence sucked the air out of the room. Conversations stopped. Heads turned. Pulse rates rose.

She worked well with her male supervisors and co-workers. She had issues with the women. They had issues with her.

Amanda practiced the art of being a "chameleon." She had the ability to change her personality, appearance, and behavior to match her surroundings.

If a client needed someone to look like Miss California and talk sports, she did it. If her date was well-read both in fiction and nonfiction, she could hold a conversation on any subject. If her date was looking for a woman who loved karaoke singing, playing pool, and going to the theater, concerts, and church, Amanda was your girl.

When she met her husband, she transformed to match his likes and dislikes. Amanda, however, hid many little lies. Little lies about where she went to school and her family background. Little lies about her dreams, hopes and wishes for her life. Little lies about favorite foods, colors, hobbies and vacation spots—places that she had never visited.

Now a year later, she admitted that she had not been honest with the man she had married. She was unhappy and afraid. If her husband found out her true background, would he leave? By living a lie, she had turned her home into Deception Central.

This chapter is about how deception can destroy trust in a relationships and how to regain trust in a marriage or relationship.

A relationship built on deception exists on a shaky foundation. Trust between husband and wife is the mortar to build a covenant marriage. Security, compatibility, honesty, forgiveness, communication skills, friendship and laughter are important elements for a forever marriage. Trust is often the virtue that is ranked the most important.

Trust is like money in the bank. It can grow with interest. It can also diminish because of too many withdrawals caused by breaches great and small. Spouses give freely when trust is listed as an asset. Dishonesty, infidelity, addictions or habits that negatively impact a relationship can erode trust. The result will be a negative balance.

Deception violates trust. It takes a lot of time and energy to maintain a lie. Like Amanda, many people live in fear that one day someone will uncover their deception. They didn't graduate from college; they didn't come from a certain family background; they are a divorcee, or they hid children that they did not raise; they had an abortion or an affair outside of marriage.

According to news reports, twenty-seven year old Lori Hacking broke down in tears when she discovered that her husband, Mark, had not graduated from the University of Utah. Furthermore, he had lied about being accepted into a medical school in North Carolina—where they were preparing to move. Lori's co-workers said she was upset about her husband's deception.

Lori and Mark argued when she confronted him. The next day, Mark contacted the police to report that Lori was missing.

Eventually, Mark was charged with murdering Lori. He pleaded guilty. He stood before the judge and admitted that he attacked his wife while she slept and later threw her body in the trash. Police retrieved her decomposing body from a landfill.

According to published reports, Jean-Claude Romand lied about his education and employment at the World Health Organization. He lied about being a doctor and about former employment at several hospitals in France. Further, he used the retirement and bonus money of friends and family in a bogus investment scheme.

It became increasing difficult for Jean-Claude to maintain his deception. He was respected and well liked, but he was afraid that people would find out his true background and identity.

In order to cover up the series of lies, Jean-Claude murdered his elderly parents in their home. He killed his wife and his two young children. He even set his own house on fire perhaps to kill himself and to cover up the deaths of his wife and children. Miraculously, according to newspapers, Jean-Claude survived the fire and was charged in the deaths of five family members. Unlike Mark Hacking or Jean-Claude Romand, most people do not go to such extremes. Thank God!

Facing false realities and correcting false information or assumptions can be traumatic. The distance between a problem and a solution can be shortened by prayer. There is nothing impossible with God.

Amanda and her husband were able to work through her past lies and deceptions. Her first step in recovery was learning how to fall in love with herself. When she learned to love herself in all of its reality, she found she could be loved for who she was rather than the person she pretended to be.

Amanda confessed and her husband forgave her. He discovered a spouse who was much more exciting. She found out that two people loved her for who she truly was—God and her husband. Her favorite scripture became: "Let the morning bring me word of your unfailing love, for I have put my trust in you. Show me the way I should go, for to you I lift up my soul." (Psalm 143:8)

Amanda was exposed to the truth of her inner being and the reality of who she was in the context of worshipping God and studying God's word. Enabled by the Holy Spirit to break the power of deception and sin, her heart was cleansed from the lies

It took time. She became comfortable with who she was and thus could relate to her husband. She had to reflect on why she fell in love with her husband in the first place. She grew to trust God, and in trusting God, she opened the door to her inner self.

Gradually, she developed confidence in God. This self-confidence produced confidence in her relationship.

She pretended to be someone else because she could not access her true self. She never took time to be the archeologist of her own personality, purpose, or plans. She could not discover who she was because she spent so much time becoming what others wanted her to be or the person someone else was looking for.

Unfortunately, there are still some people who believe that the only way they can get men and women to the altar or in the bedroom are through tricks and traps. Pregnancies, false pregnancies, phony backgrounds, bogus schemes, grandiose promises, false confessions of love, alcohol, drugs and rape are some of the traps. Like Amanda, some are not so obvious yet they are just as devious.

Amanda had what she wanted but was unhappy because she got it the wrong way. We often create "that someone" we want to be to get "that someone" who we want to be with. We carefully craft a person with a matching wardrobe and lifestyle whether we can afford it or not. A lot of time is spent on the external, ignoring the internal.

Like Leah, in due season, we could wake up disappointed. She was with the right man but she was the wrong woman. The right fish was caught with the wrong bait.

Rachel ended up being the "other woman" because of the deception orchestrated by her father. She may or may not have been a willing participant, but nevertheless, she was a part of a terrible deception.

Jacob had already been through one wedding week. Is it possible that he comes tired to Rachel's wedding tent after having satiated his desires with Leah?

Monogamous married relationships are as old as Adam and Eve and the Garden of Eden. The narrator of Genesis speaks of polygamy beginning in Genesis 4:19. Often, polygamy was more trouble than it was worth.

Polygamy often bore jealousy, conflict, trouble and sin. Read the scriptures about Abraham, Sarah, and Hagar, and David, Solomon, and Gideon (Genesis 21; Judges 8:29–9:57; 2 Samuel 11, 13; 1 Kings 11:1–8). Ancient people were warned against this practice in Deuteronomy 17:17.

According to some scholars, one of the reasons given for the rise of polygamy was the importance of the family legacy. Children were important to carry on the family name and to maintain family possessions. Oftentimes, if a woman was childless, her slave or household servant would be given to the husband. The husband would birth children through the surrogate mother. In a few African cultures, when children are born through adulterous relationships, the offspring belongs to the family of the wayward husband. The wife then raises the love child of her husband. In ancient times, the offspring from the husband and the concubine would carry all the rights and privileges of an heir.

Abraham and Sarah participated in this Mesopotamian custom. Later on, both Leah and Rachel gave their handmaids to Jacob. The children born "on the side" were full-fledged members of the family.

There are some scholars who believe that the concern for procreation was not at the root of this love triangle between Jacob and Rachel and Leah. This arrangement was a by-product of deception and manipulation. Laban married off two daughters to the best available male who could further his ambitions of wealth and power.

Fredericka and Carlos were in love, and while in their late twenties, they exchanged marriage vows. In college, Fredericka was a talented basketball player. She continued to play for a community team even though she injured her knee in her senior year.

Ordinary weekly games didn't challenge her old injury. It only occurred during the seasonal league playoffs when her team played several games during the week and on weekends. The increased number of games hampered Fredericka's performance.

In order to make it through, she relied on pain pills. She started out on OxyContin. In a few days, she was hooked. The season was over but she continued getting prescriptions for a nonexisting knee pain. She was spending hundreds of dollars for OxyContin and Lortab.

Their insurance coverage was maxed out and the company would no longer pay for the prescriptions. Her husband became concerned. Fredericka lied to him and told him that she was no longer taking the pills. Physically, she was fine.

In order to support her growing addiction to opiates, Fredericka secretly dipped into the couple's savings account. She borrowed money from friends, teammates and co-workers. She pawned her jewelry—even her wedding ring. She told her husband that someone had stolen it from her locker during a game.

She went from doctor to doctor to get new prescriptions and even sought the pain pills over the Internet. The secrecy was killing Fredericka. One night, she became overwhelmed and began to cry uncontrollably. Carlos wasn't sure what was going on but he had a suspicion.

Carlos came home one evening from work and found his wife bent over with severe body cramping. She had tried to stop taking the pills on her own but had become violently ill. All day, she had been sick with diarrhea and was sweating profusely. He rushed her to the emergency room.

Doctors confirmed that she was in withdrawal from an opiate addiction. There were expensive rapid detoxification treatments but most were controversial and were not covered by insurance companies.

There was no quick cure. Her road to recovery was going to be long.

Fredericka believed her husband would walk out on her when she confessed all the sordid details of the past few years. She knew he would leave her when she found out how much money she owed and that their savings gone.

Carlos was angry and frustrated. He was tired of the lies and the secrets. He wasn't sure he could ever trust her with money ever again. He
wondered if he would ever be able to take her at her word.

He was also embarrassed. How do you explain to their parents,
friends and co-workers that your wife abused prescription drugs? This is
not what he signed on for when he stood with her in their little country
church and vowed "in sickness and in health."

Fredericka could barely look Carlos in the eyes. She fed her guilt
with recrimination statements. "I'm no good. I'm hopeless. I let you
down. I won't blame you if you leave me!"

Carlos vented his anger on a vending machine outside the family
waiting room. He told the machine everything he felt, from betrayal to
rage. He ticked off a list of lies while he kicked the machine at each in-
fraction. When hospital security came to investigate the noise, Carlos
was sitting beside the machines quietly weeping.

Stan and I arrived at the hospital and had prayer with Carlos. We sat
in the waiting room while Fredericka was transferred from the emergency room to a rehabilitation ward. We sat in silence while we watched
God work on the heart of the man who was still a babe in Christ.

The emergency room physicians came to explain Fredericka's treat-
ment strategy to Carlos. She may have gotten hooked over night but
healing was going to take time. Healing required his support and partic-
ipation.

Carlos wanted to see his wife alone. After spending a few minutes
alone with his wife, he requested that we join them for prayer. He begged
her family to also wait.

When Stan and I walked into the room, Carlos was lying beside his
wife. He was rocking her. He was hugging her. He was telling her they
would make it through . . . together!

We signaled to Carlos that we would see them in the morning. We
said a silent prayer over them and left the couple to reconcile with each
other and with God.

Kendra and Damien's marriage didn't survive the network of lies and
deception that were created to cover up a gambling addiction. They were
a mature couple with grown children who were looking forward to their
retirement years together.

At their luxurious suburban home, I was invited to officiate their
twenty-fifth wedding anniversary in the presence of a host of children,

grandchildren, family and friends. As a surprise gift, their children gave them an all-expense-paid second honeymoon. This was a well-traveled couple and there weren't many places they had not visited. It was a challenge but they all agreed that Reno, Nevada, was the place to go.

Their family insisted that they leave all their old foggy ways behind them. They were to take only the basic necessities like socks, underwear, and pajamas. They were given several thousand dollars in gift money to buy a new 21st century wardrobe, hairstyle and haircut.

The couple started out shopping together but Damien didn't have the patience to go from shop to shop. Kendra went from shopping to the spa for a variety of treatments for the body, face and hair. Damien went to the casinos.

Kendra returned to their room freshly painted and pampered. She was looking forward to a leisurely evening of dining and dancing. She purchased a little black dress that complimented her full bodied figure. She said she showed a little too much but just enough to make Damien want to order room service and call it a night.

Damien didn't show. She called his cell phone. He didn't answer repeated calls or return her messages. She finally went down into the hotel restaurant and then into the casino, thinking he had simply lost track of time.

Kendra found him at the poker table. He was laughing and joking with his tablemates. There were a stack of chips in front of him.

Damien yelled for her to come over and sit next to him. He told her to have a seat. He whispered in her ear that as long as she played, she could get free drinks. It was obvious he had had one to many. She asked him where the money came from and he shushed her into silence.

Kendra knew nothing about poker and got up from her seat. She said it was time for dinner and encouraged her husband to take her to dinner. He refused. He said he was on a winning streak and would join her in the restaurant.

This was not like the Damien she had known for twenty-five years. Yes, they had come to have fun but fun together in an activity that wasn't in conflict with their faith. Had he been like this all along? Had she been too busy with the children and her career and missed it?

Kendra waited. She finally ordered her dinner. She ate alone in her new dress, with her new hair style and painted nails that Damien hadn't even notice. She was alone that night and the rest of the weekend.

Damien contented himself with poker, the roulette wheel and the crap table. He told her he never felt a rush like he felt when he won money. He didn't tell her he also felt a rush when he lost, but since it wasn't their money he really didn't care.

When the supposed second honeymoon was over, Kendra was relieved because she believed the gambling was just a momentary menopausal knee-jerk response. Perhaps this was Damien's version of a mid-life crisis. Never fear, they lived in a state where casino gambling was not permitted.

It didn't end. Damien started to gamble on the Internet. It particularly hurt Kendra because she was the one who insisted that he learn to use the Internet so they could e-mail their grandchildren.

During all hours of the night and day, Kendra would catch Damien playing Texas Hold 'em poker or Vegas style roulette. He never expressed a desire to go to horse races but now from their home, he was betting on them all over the country.

Damien had gotten so good with online gambling that he discovered a site where he could create his own avatar complete with facial expressions and gestures. The figures were not real. They would just sit around the poker table but he could bring a real life component to the fantasy game.

Unlike substance abuse, people can hide a gambling addiction. There is no overdose per se until you start losing more money than you win. The overdose comes when you choose gambling over your regular life.

Damien made excuses. He said he could stop whenever he wanted. It wasn't a habit but something to do now that he had retired. He wasn't losing more than they could bear.

Kendra missed her husband. She had waited twenty-five years for him to retire so she could have his undivided attention. He was now more interested in Internet gambling than her. She slowly watched their relationship erode because of his addiction to gambling.

There were many and daily confrontations and accusations. She enlisted the help of her children but even that didn't work. She tried to talk him through it but he refused to listen. Kendra pleaded screamed, cried, preached, slung scripture at him and made threats. Nothing seemed to work.

When one of her daughters suggested a gambling anonymous group, Kendra wouldn't listen. The embarrassment about his gambling problem was greater than the embarrassment over marital discord. She needed help but wouldn't seek help outside the family unit.

Damien hit a brick wall the day Kendra found out that he had gambled away their life savings including the nest egg they had saved for emergencies such as long-term medical care, prescriptions or treatments not covered by Medicaid or Medicare. He also had begun to dip into their investments. The next day she filed for divorce.

Is there hope for us, even when we sow seeds of our own destruction?

Satan, as the father of lies, distorts our understanding of the word of God. Anything which diverges from the truth of God's word is a lie. Up to a point, often it is easier to live the lie than to embrace the truth.

Lies and deceptions are built into a marriage using big blocks of deceit, shame, secrecy and a distortion of reality. People often will fight to keep things a secret rather than seek help. Look at the actions of Kendra and Amanda or Mark and Jean-Claude. The wall can be scaled with reconciliation. We can all repent and allow the Holy Spirit into our hearts as did Fredericka and Carlos. The wall can be broken down by the truth of God's word. It is the truth that indeed provides freedom.

"Rather, we have renounced secret and shameful ways; we do not use deception, nor do we distort the word of God. On the contrary, by setting forth the truth plainly we commend ourselves to every man's conscience in the sight of God." (2 Corinthians 4:2)

Building trust begins with confession. God is faithful to forgive us all of our sins when we confess. (1 John 1:9)

The prophet Nathan confronted David about his adulterous behavior with Bathsheba. David tried to cover his sin with a deception that went wild. He seduced the next door neighbor and got her pregnant. He tried to arrange a coverup by bringing her husband, Uriah, home from the front line of war. The husband was more loyal to the king than his need to lie with his wife.

Uriah went back to war, where David instructed that he be placed in harms way. The husband died in battle.

David's confession, a humble prayer for cleansing and forgiveness, is found in Psalm 51. He prays with a contrite heart by using words like mercy, unfailing love, great compassion, wash, cleanse and blot out.

He paints an image of God with a papyrus scroll of his life and asks God to blot out his transgressions. He requests cleansing as one would clean a filthy rag. He wanted to be made clean in the sight of God. He realizes that he has sinned against God and has acted contrary to what he's been taught and what he knows to be God's desires.

David requests that God create in him a pure heart, a willing spirit and an unwavering faithfulness to serve. Joy would return to his soul. David requested that God not remove the Spirit from him that had equipped him to serve in the royal office. This could be a reflection upon when God withdrew his support from Saul. his predecessor.

Confession to God comes first. Forgiveness is promised by God's word—then go and sin no more. If you need help from a pastor, pastoral counselor, psychiatrist or support group, get it!

Consider confessing to your spouse, especially if the thorn in your flesh distorts your reality, is illegal, or dangerous to you or your spouse. Do you have a problem with gambling, Internet gambling, abusing prescription drugs, Internet pornography, habitual lying, living a fantasy life or frittering away family finances?

Emily never knew her husband struggled with a pornography problem until she walked into their bedroom one night. She found him reading an X-rated magazine. She didn't know this had been a problem that he had wrestled with since his teen years. Habitually, he would steal his father's magazines and hide them in his room.

Judgment seat sitting is often a popular pastime. Beloved church-going people of God wrestled with some of the same issues as do those outside of the faith. Therefore, don't be so quick to say it is a "them" issue because is also an "us" issue. We are subject to the same temptations and we have all fallen short of the glory of God.

We can no longer afford to act like ostriches with our "heads in the sand" response. There are other critical and controversial issues such as confronting the HIV/AIDS pandemic. We can become our own worse enemy when we are silent and secret about what can harm, hurt and kill. Martin Luther King Jr. once said that there comes a time when silence is betrayal.

The first confession is to God. The second is to your partner. "Confess your sins to each other and pray for each other so they you may be healed. . . ." (James 5:16)

Prayer is a mighty tool in the arsenal of the believer. While Fredericka was in rehab, before going home every night, Carlos would climb into bed to pray over Fredericka. At first, she resisted. Gradually she began to look forward to their evening prayer sessions. He would hug her close and pray out loud his love for her and God. He asked God to use the medical staff and facility as an instrument to heal her and their relationship. He prayed that God would supply all her needs so that she wouldn't depend on a high from prescription drugs.

When she was out of rehab, Carlos nightly continued to snuggle next to her, always asking God to bless her. He began to ask God for specific requests. As God began to answer the prayers, one night Fredericka rededicated her life to Jesus Christ.

Carlos later confided to Fredericka that in the beginning, he was determined to help the healing process by monitoring her behavior day and night. It was during one of those nightly prayer vigils that God told him not to imprison his wife for something that God had already forgiven.

In the *Power of a Praying Wife*, Stormie Omaritan writes that amazing things happen when we pray for another person. We enter into the presence of God and are filled with God's Spirit of love. Hardness melts and we are able to forgive when we get beyond the hurts.

There is no getting around the fact that what happens to them also happens to you, she indicates. Pray for yourself and your spouse so that you do not miss out on the blessing and fulfillment you both want.

Now, Aunt Agony would tell you that the stuff that's dead and over with ought to stay buried. It should never see the light of day again. If it is not dead and stands between you and your partner, ask God for guidance or consult a professional Christian counselor.

The next step to restore trust in a relationship is repentance. The gospel of Mark records the first message of Christ as the call to repentance. The trumpet blast that announces Jesus' presence is given by John the Baptist. He issued a call for the people to repent for God's Realm was at hand.

Repentance is more than a tidal wave of remorse or deep conviction of sin. The literal translation for the Greek word for repentance means "to change the mind." It means to shift one's thinking into reverse, much like the gears of an automobile shifting from first to second and third.

When we repent, our thinking demonstrates the introduction of new information about God. We begin to re-orient our life in reference to God's purpose, will, and word.

Repentance is a decision that indicates an inward change with external implication. In Luke 19, the tax collector Zacchaeus repents after the visitation of Christ to his home in Jericho. He changes his mind about God and himself. The greedy tax collector becomes a generous philanthropist, the taker becomes a giver, the community liability becomes an asset, and the servant of mammon becomes a servant of God.

It would be the reunion between Jacob and Esau—several years in the future—before we would see any repentance from Jacob. There is shock, upset and disappointment but little repentance, which will be explored in the next chapter.

Repent, beloved. Let nothing exist between your souls and your Savior. We reap what we sow yet there are some seeds we do not ever want to sprout. We trust God to respond to our confession and repentance with forgiveness.

We are judged guilty but we still throw ourselves upon the mercy of the courts. It is because of the Lord's mercies that we are not consumed by the consequences of our behavior. (Lamentations 3:22) God still provides new mercies with the rising of the sun. (Lamentations 3:23)

As we experience forgiveness from God, we must also learn to forgive those who have manipulated our affections, tricked us or mistreated our trust. Forgiveness doesn't mean we allow them to do it again. It means we release them from the debt.

Amanda was pleasantly shocked when her husband forgave her. He wanted to start all over again from courtship to lovers to friendship. He set up a date at a restaurant of her choice and began with the introductions: "What is your name? What do you do for a living?"

Today is a good day to ask God to help us release those who have lied or deceived us. It doesn't matter whether or not they have confessed to God or to you from the debt they owe. Remember Christ has released us from our debts.

If your life is in danger, you can still forgive. You will have to face the reality that it may be too dangerous for you to continue the relationship.

We must never forget that by God's grace, we can put aside our right to punish them for their wrong—even when we want their wrong to be returned to them. God has not given that privilege to us. Vengeance belongs to God.

Repentance is not a threat but an open invitation to "Come all ye who are heavy laden and Christ will give us rest." It is an invitation to call upon the God's name and be saved. It is an invitation to come out of the shadow of deception and into the light of truth.

Repentance is an invitation to look at the cross of Calvary and recognize God's love for you. It is your invitation to gaze at the empty tomb to realize Christ has conquered the father of lies, sin, death, and hell. It is an invitation to trust God and lean not unto your own understanding.

"I have no greater joy than to hear that my children are walking in the truth." (3 John 4)

Living the truth often takes courage because some of us have a hard time admitting that we have a weakness, fault or sin. We may have a hard time facing our own humanity or we would rather be what we are not.

God rejoices when we embrace the truth. If you stumble, get back up. If you slip, try again. If you can't do it alone, get help. If an obstacle is in your path, jump over it.

Just make sure you see far enough ahead. There is a story about a little boy, his birthday and a lot of rain in a dry place. The community suffered from a drought and the people prayed. Prayers were answered on this little boy's birthday and it upset him. It seemed God could have chosen a better day on which to rain other than on my birthday, he thought. He looked forward to fishing on the lake. It was to be his birthday treat with his dad.

He moped around the house all day. His parents tried to sooth him with alternate suggestions such as the rain is going to stop or if the rain didn't stop today he could go the next day. The rain was needed and there were still other fun things to do on his birthday. Nothing improved his mood.

He felt that God had betrayed him. God had deliberately messed up what he had looked forward to for so long. Kendra blamed God for allowing her second honeymoon and retirement to be messed up by a mid-life gambling problem.

Later in the day, the clouds cleared, the sun came out and the boy and his father packed their gear and headed for the lake. The fish were biting and it became the best birthday ever.

That evening, his father showed him how to clean fish and his mother prepared them for his birthday dinner. The little boy asked to say the grace.

"Lord, forgive me for being moody and moping around the house earlier today. I was very angry," prayed the boy. "I just couldn't see far enough ahead."

Be sure to see far enough ahead.

S.M.A.R.T. MOVES
(Spiritual Motivation for Action and Real Transformation)

Talking Points

1. Have you ever deceived someone to gain an advantage in a relationship or a job?

2. Have you ever been deceived in a relationship? Describe how you felt.

3. In what ways can you defuse Deception Central in your home, church or office?

4. If you are in a relationship, sit down and discuss ways to keep the lines of communication open to build trust.

5. Do you think couples should keep secrets from each other? If so, why? If not, are you prepared to hear the truth?

6. Do you need help in an area of your life and failed to get it?

7. Have you ever lied about your past to your spouse?

The Word of Prayer

Dear God, if I am being deceived, in the name of Jesus, reveal it to me. Give me courage to face it and to cease being a partner of deception. In Jesus' name. Amen.

Parent God, help me to forgive my spouse for keeping harmful secrets from me. Create in him a clean heart, O God, and renew a right spirit within me. I take back the stolen intimacy and trust in my marriage so that together, we can live in the fullness and power of your love. In Jesus' name. Amen.

"Let the morning bring word of your unfailing love, for I have put my trust in you. Show me the way I should go, for to you I lift up my soul." (Psalm 143:8)

The Word of God

Lord Jesus, help me to renounce any secret and shameful ways. Help me to stand firm with the belt of truth around me and the breastplate of righteousness in place. When I stray from your word, send those who will lovingly help me and instruct me to live in freedom. In Jesus' name. Amen.

Foreplay

This morning, agree to become partners in health and wholeness. Share information and inspiration that helps you strengthen each other.

Pillow Talk

Let your spouse know that you pray that they do not have to lie to make you love them.

Kiss and Tell

Remind the love of your life that your marriage is worth the effort it takes for the both of you to prosper and be in good health. (3 John 2)

Kiss and Make Up

This is to remind Mr. and Mrs. Right All the Time that we all make mistakes. Be sure to see far enough ahead to navigate your relationship out of shallow waters and around the rocks that can rip it apart. Sail towards the peaceful waters of forgiveness and reconciliation.

Marital Madness

Creating a prison for your spouse where he must report every move and action to you 24 hours a day puts your relationship into ICU. In spite of the lies and deception, explore the depths of your relationship and develop a new plan based on mutual trust and support.

Singularity

If you begin a relationship built on an illusion, image, lie or false résumé, you are not ready for a relationship. Get to know God and who God says you are. Get to know yourself before you pursue a covenant commitment.

SIX

DOWN BUT NOT OUT

When the Lord saw that Leah was not loved . . .

Genesis 29:31

*The most terrible poverty is loneliness
and the feeling of being unloved.*

Mother Teresa

Shopping with new grandmothers can be an exceptional experience. I spent a few hours navigating children's stores with a friend who had been blessed with a granddaughter.

The child was at the cute and cuddly stage. She learned how to call the one who gave her lots of attention "ganma." As she walked, she waddled because of her big plastic diaper. Pulling up on the furniture, she named and claimed everything that was not nailed down in the environment. In this unique boutique she found a tiny pink ballerina outfit complete with a tulle tutu. New "ganma" purchased it for her little darling along with a crown.

I asked her why she would purchase something so frivolous. She responded that the parents never purchase anything beyond the basic necessities. She did it because every princess needs a wardrobe and a crown. She wanted her granddaughter to learn how to wear her crown before the world tried to tell her that she was not royalty. If she did not believe she was special or had something to give, she would always take what was given to her without question. She was beginning the journey towards coming of age.

Have you noticed this little detail about living? We are either coming of age or coming to terms with the life we have been given.

We are coming of age—coming into life, growing up, evolving and learning how to play the hand that we have been dealt!

We were coming in. We are waiting for a magic moment, a mysterious time when we will be ushered into where the game will be played, into the huddle where the plays will be called and the decisions made.

We were coming of age. Half our lives are spent in a steady dance with life—a tango where life grabs us and drags us across the prepubescence dance floor. Some of us lost our innocence while listening to our parents' Moms Mabley and Redd Foxx records found hidden in the basement; today, our children lose their innocence on the Internet.

Everything was so new then—the fresh flush of emotions, fear, anger, joy and pain, sunshine and rain, happiness, sympathy and compassion. It was all so new. In the newness, we only had someone's word about what it was all about, somebody's testimony about when it happened to them.

All of a sudden things began to happen to us that have happened to boys and girls for eons. We changed. We began a hormonal roller coaster ride that took us from adolescence to adulthood not determined by the chronological tick of the clock but by the kiros timing of God. Since it was all so new, we didn't know what to do with it. We said we did but we lied.

We were coming of age. We were coming in tight skirts, blue eye shadow and listening to 45 rpm records. The men in our lives were the Platters, the Dells, the Temptations, Smokey Robinson and the Miracles, Curtis Mayfield and the Impressions, Harold Melvin and the Blue Notes. We were coming in with Martha Reeves and the Vandellas' hit song "Dancing in the Streets." We wore brogans, saddle oxfords or high top tennis shoes. We wanted to be grown enough to drive a "deuce and a quarter"—that is a Buick Electra 225.

We had afros and afro puffs, and later there were fades. We were coming in. The women in our lives were Aretha Franklin, Chaka Khan, Patti LaBelle and the Bluebells, Tina Turner, and Diana Ross.

Our dance was the twist and shout. Our line dance was not the Electric Slide but the Madison. Back in the day, our style was hot pants and patent leather boots, as in these boots were made for walking.

Our poet was Nikki Giovanni, our play was *For Colored Girls Who Have Considered Suicide/When the Rainbow is Enuf.* Our protest was nonviolent and our shout was "Black Power!"

We were coming in. We shut down universities and stared down the National Guard. We broke the color line—being the first to be bussed across town to be somebody's first African American experience. We sat down at lunch counters, movie theaters, school houses and sidewalks in the name of Civil Rights. Like prisoners of war, we took the water hoses and dogs.

Our war was Vietnam. Our theme was, "The Revolution Will Not Be Televised." Our movie was *Uptown Saturday Night.* Our girl was Foxy Brown and our hero was Shaft, played by Richard Roundtree.

We were coming of age in a changing world. Now the present has become the past and the future has become the present. What was is now. What can be, is still coming.

We have come of age. We have seen too much and done too many things. We knew better and should have done better but as soon as we became competent, we had to change and adapt to a new reality.

Now we had to come to terms with the life we had. We had to play the hand we were dealt.

Leah had come of age and had to deal with her own new set of realities. She had to come to terms with the life she had. Could it be that she was in love with a man who had no intention of loving her in return?

She had no voice, no power, and no say. Secluded and subdued, she submitted to the indignity of living with a man, knowing all along he preferred her sister.

Ask Leah how she felt living with Jacob during her wedding week. She was rejected on her wedding morning, unwanted and unloved by her new husband, by her father and even by herself. She didn't love herself enough to say no to the deception devised by her father. Cultural customs may have prevented any hint of refusal.

Perhaps she felt as betrayed as Jacob. Betrayal strikes at the heart and makes us vulnerable to the world. We have been hurt by the one we hoped would care enough not to hurt us.

Leah was trapped. She was a weed. "A weed," says Ella Wilcox, "is but an unloved flower." Leah was stigmatized because it was said that she had "weak eyes" in comparison to the beautiful floral display that belonged to her sister Rachel. Leah's identity was derailed.

In *The Secret of Significance,* Robert S. McGee describes four ways in which our identity can be derailed. If we want to feel good about ourselves, we must perform at a certain level. Anything less than perfection is unacceptable. We must be approved by those who we believe are important to us. We will grab whatever face or space we can in an effort to get what is needed. If we do not receive others' approval, we feel unworthy. We blame ourselves for failure and believe that we deserve to be punished.

In spite of outward appearances, Leah was a failure. Somebody had to be tricked into marrying her. The relationship was forced. Publicly, she was a mockery. She was known as the bride who had performed her duties because "the bridegroom completed her week." I wonder why it was her week and not their week or his week. Privately, Jacob wanted Rachel, but nevertheless he took Leah.

Leah was a disposable woman. Disposable women are those women who resemble disposable diapers, trash bags, paper towels, tissues or "to go" containers. They are used and thrown away. They are not treated like fine china reserved for special occasions. They are not treasured like crystal stemware or cherished like heirlooms loved by each succeeding generation.

Disposable women are like everyday dishes. They are kept even when they are worn, chipped or scratched.

Disposable women are the one night stands, casual sexual relationships, or nighttime wonders that are shunned during the day. They are treated royally after midnight and like pariahs before dawn. Men seek them out at the club or only think about them when they become drunk.

In a study done as a part of a Next Generation Program, the Marriage Project heard a variety of responses about how men meet women. The time and place of the meeting had a lot to do with a man's intentions and his expectations of a relationship. Women met in bars or dance clubs were not necessarily considered "marriage material." They were thought of as casual sex partners. By walking across a crowded dance floor, a woman could have "been hit on" by several men before an introduction is actually made. The standards for a live-in girlfriend are different from the "soul mate" men eventually want to marry. The prospective live-in girlfriend occupies a lower rating on the "marriage meter." She is a "second best partner." She provides convenient sexual relations, shared economies and a means to avoid a divorce—especially since there is no marriage. Thus, she is a disposable woman or the live-in housekeeper who keeps everything straight until the real soul mate comes along.

In the book of Esther, Queen Vashti could probably be considered a disposable woman. Her husband sent for her after he had been in a drunken debauchery for 120 days. While only wearing her crown, Vashti was asked by King Xereus to display her naked body to his companions. Perhaps he was engaged in the ageless game of "mine is better than yours."

When she failed to perform at the level of his expectation, she was banished from the country. Vashti was disposed while the ruler played his version of the reality show *The Bachelor.* Younger women were brought before Xereus. Hadassah walked away with more than a rose. She got a crown.

Leah was trapped and wounded. Many times our wounding comes early in life, especially if all we want is the attention of a parent. But it never comes. We want to dance with our daddies and he never comes. We want to do the "look at me" routine but no one looks. She would either have to get sick or achieve great things to get a speck of attention.

Leah was not the preferred daughter who was expected to bring honor and glory to the family. She was not favored or adored by her father. Obviously, she was not favored by history. She was a princess without appreciation.

Every day, Lennie's mother told her that she was neither expected nor wanted. The pregnancy was a mistake and not getting an abortion was a mistake. Now, the mother was weighed down with a kid that she resented.

Lennie was treated as an afterthought. As such, Lennie learned at an early age to take care of Lennie. She knew if she didn't find any food, she wouldn't eat. If she didn't learn to clean herself or her room, she'd live in filth.

When Lennie's mother saw that Lennie could be useful, she forced her to be her servant. Lennie cooked the meals and took care of the house—whatever her mother needed. It was the least Lennie could do, since in her mother's words she was "a worthless piece of crap."

It dawned on Lennie that if she kept the house perfectly clean, her mother would love her. Lennie scrubbed floors, washed and ironed clothes, and cooked meals. She waited to hear at least one "thank you" or "good job Lennie." But it never happened.

Arriving home early after taking a final exam and excited about her approaching graduation, Lennie returned to an empty house. Her mother was gone. Closets and drawers were empty. There was no note. There was no goodbye. She was simply and definitely gone.

Lennie carried her overwhelming desire to please and meet the approval of others into her first marriage. She thought if she did everything Jimmy wanted, he would love her and never leave her. Whenever Jimmy was late or forgot to lavish praise on Lennie for ironing his shirts or doing some outstanding achievement on her job, she would accuse him of not loving her. Tired of the tears and tirades, Jimmy left.

Lennie wanted to hurt him as much as she was hurt. She wanted to pick up something and go after him.

Aunt Agony says it is okay to feel like you want to hurt someone. Many times, she's felt like murdering someone and causing mayhem. It is one thing to think it and another thing to do it. Of course, it is wrong to carry out destructive behavior.

In a January, 2004, *Newsweek* article titled "12 Things You Must Know to Survive and Thrive in America," Ellis Cose addressed several issues of interest to African Americans His twelfth mantra applied to men and women of every kindred and tribe. He wrote, "Don't force innocent others to bear the price of your pain."

In a sermon about the aftermath of Hurricane Katrina, I said that especially in this postmodern 21st century era, one of the challenges in any life, in any age, and at any time is to bring closure to issues and events that have damaged our body, mind or spirit. We find it difficult to turn the page, complete the chapter, start another one or even close the book altogether!

We stumbled to bring closure to traumatic experiences, closure to devastating incidents, and closure to events that challenge our comfort zones and rock our worlds.

Oftentimes, it remains an open issue because, it, he, she or they may be finished with us but we are not finished with them. The book remains open! Everyone has had their say but us—or we have not found the courage to let it go.

Over time, the wound never heals because we continue to pick at the scar. We are not ready to close the matter and we want an unrealistic ending. We remove the bandage too soon, exposing the wound to more germs and possible infection from the same source that wounded it.

Regretfully, we live with the hope that in spite of what has already transpired, another benediction can be pronounced.

On the other hand, we fail to bring closure because others will not leave it alone. As far as you are concerned, it is over. They (and you know who they are) talk about it around your social circle, they post it online, and they remind you of every finite detail until it reappears on your emotional radar screen. Before you know it, it starts to make appearances in your consciousness. It begins to take starring roles in your daydreams and nightmares.

There are some who are crisis junkies. Closure is not in our vocabulary! We just don't feel right unless there is a crisis going on! A day is not productive until there's an upset somewhere!

Some people thrive on crises. They feed upon the tentacles that threaten to unravel their sanity or someone else's sanity. They relish a good crisis where they either play the role of the victim or they play the role of the perpetrator.

In the medical field, to close a simple wound simply requires a bandage. This is an appropriate covering with disinfectant or ointments that will promote healing. A more complex wound requires closure with the use of sutures, or stitches. The wound is closed and in a few weeks even the sutures disappear.

If the problem persists, than the medical technician reopens the wound. They scrape away the infection, drain away impurities, and cleanse the wound. The opening is then closed.

Reopening old wounds can be as devastating as the original wound. The replay button is pushed and everything that had been forgotten is once again alive and in living color. This is what happened to Lennie. She could not stop playing the reruns of her childhood.

There are times when opening old wounds is necessary. Unless the poison is removed, a greater problem could occur. What affected only one area could spread to others—contaminating other portions of your life.

Wounds can be the womb through which stress related disorders are born, the place where the sperm of anger meets the seed of hatred and rage is birthed. Buried rage is powerful. When that animal is loosed, writes George McKinney, it doesn't care about consequences. It only cares only about retribution.

Wounds can also be a source of healing. It is weakness converted into strength with the experience becoming a source of strength, as in Jesus was wounded for our transgression and bruised for our iniquity.

Leah had to live with the new rules of her new relationship. Rachel was loved. Leah was not. Rachel was adorned. Leah was not. Rachel was the queen to Jacob's king. Leah was the princess without appreciation. Rachel was chosen. Leah was an obligation. Rachel was the soul mate. Leah was the live-in sex partner.

Every relationship has rules whether they are stated, understated, written or unspoken. These rules govern affiliations and connections among the human family. These rules, like them or not, codify behavior, actions and activities. There are rules of relationship between spouses, parents and their children, siblings, friends and enemies.

Everyone lives with a set of silent rules. Couples often do not talk about them unless an unspoken rule is broken, according to Drs. Les and Leslie Parrott in *Saving Your Marriage Before it Starts.*

When the unspoken rule is broken, the "breakee" is frustrated because they didn't know that they had done something wrong. The rule maker is frustrated because the "breakee" should have known what to do. In a relationship, it is assumed that everyone shares the same expectations even though they come from different experiences. In order to identify the unspoken rules, it is as if each partner must become an amateur mind reader or have the gift of discernment.

Aunt Agony says, "What you say is what you get. What you don't say is what you don't get." She also says, "I can read lips and body language, especially if it is a good looking body. I don't read minds. How can you expect me to follow a road I don't know is there?!"

Unspoken rules can run the gamut. When and how will the bills be paid? Who will handle the morning routines? Who will be responsible for maintaining toiletries like the toothpaste and toilet paper? Who is going to be honest about taboo subjects like weight gain, exercise and ex's of any type?

Kit grew up in a house of open doors. The only closed door was the bathroom door—and that was only closed when it was occupied. She married a man who grew up in a house of closed doors. You never opened one without knocking first.

Imagine Kit's surprise when she walked into the bathroom to put on her make up. Her husband was shocked. He told her she had disrespected him. He had never shared the unspoken rules about open and closed doors.

Arlene went to Ron's family reunion. She was meeting her fiancé's family for the first time. After the round of initial introductions, she began a conversation with Ron's sister with the question, "When is the baby due?"

His sister looked pregnant. She, however, was not pregnant. She was very well-endowed, wearing a kaftan to cover her full-figure.

Suddenly, the room grew silent. Ron's sister left the room in tears. Arlene was at a loss for words. She didn't know why her questions had caused so much pain.

Arlene broke the family's unspoken rule. You do not inquire about someone's weight, body mass or dress size. Arlene was embarrassed and her fiancé was mortified. To this day, the sister doesn't speak to her.

Randy married Maize. The wedding was a lavish affair. Family and friends flew in from all parts of the world. Gifts were stacked on multiple tables and everyone had a wonderful time.

At the reception, Randy went back to the buffet to load his plate up again. While there he met a man who said he was Maize's real father. Randy was surprised and called to his new bride to come to the other side of the room where he was. He wanted to see if she knew her father was there.

Randy had no idea that the man who had identified himself as his wife's real father was persona non gratas. Her stepfather took exception to his presence in a very vocal way.

By the time the argument was over, Maize was in tears. She blamed Randy for ruining her wedding. He didn't know the silent rule about Maize's father, the wedding crasher.

The Bible teaches that what governs our relationship with our parents is honor. Honor your father and mother that your days may be long on the earth. In our relationship with our children, we are to treasure and train a child in the way the child should go. Our children are to obey their parents. A man must leave his parents for a wife. Husbands are to love their wives like Christ loved the church and love their wives as they love their own bodies. Wives are to honor and respect their husbands and we are to love God with all of our heart, mind and soul.

We are to love our neighbor as ourselves. Neighborly love is not an exclusive rule for co-workers, church members and casual acquaintances. It is for those closest to you and those who are far away.

In our relationship with God, we like to believe there are relational rules. If we love God, we will keep God's commandants. As God's disciples, we are to be known by our love. God will reward those who diligently seek God. Love your sister and brother whom you have seen like the God whom you haven't seen.

If we humble ourselves and turn from our wicked ways, God promises to hear our prayers, and heal the land. If we confess our sins, God will be faithful to forgive. If we give, it shall be given. If we call upon the name of God, we shall be saved. And faith without works is a dead issue.

In our relationship with God, there are expectations on both sides of the track. Micha provided the most memorable statement in the Hebrew Bible defining a proper relationship with God. Perhaps he drew from his contemporaries, Hosea, Amos and Isaiah, to remind us that this God relationship requires us to act justly and to love mercy and to walk humbly with God.

We expect God to respond. We surely desire a positive response to our queries and cries for help.

The Israelites prayed that God would initiate an evacuation scenario in the wake of 400 years of bondage in Egypt. Solomon prayed for and received wisdom to rule God's people. God did it.

We expect God to answer our prayers with assured positive outcomes. We seldom expect a negative response or no response.

But (you should have known there would be a but) in spite of the rules of relationship or what we expect God to do or in spite of the closeness or how tight we feel we are with God, there are times when God chooses to answer right away or in the way we do not expect. At worse we are angry and at best we are disappointed.

Abraham prayed that God would spare Sodom and Gomorrah. God didn't. David prayed that his illicit love child by another man's wife would survive. The child died. Jesus prayed that the bitter cup would pass from him. It didn't. Paul, who loved God, had gifts of prophecy. He planted churches. He commanded the language like a poet and had authority in his voice. Yet, when he prayed for a thorn to be removed, God said God's grace was sufficient.

All of the events were going on in Leah's life and yet not a word from God.

Job also prayed but his children were killed. His cattle were destroyed. His health failed. His wife was a discouraging presence and his friends condemned him.

Trials knocked on his door. Disease covered his body. Sorrow ripped his spirit and grief gripped his heart. Misery called and depression cast a midnight shadow. But God was silent.

In his dealing with what life handed him, Job cried out to God, "Give me some advocate that can stand between you and me and draw us together." God didn't say a mumbling word.

The silence of God has been described as one of the many issues on Calvary's Hill. As Jesus bore the sins of the whole world, the sun was silent and hid its face. Uncharacteristically, the sky darkened while darkness covered the earth. The earth rumbled its disapproval. The only cries were from those persons left at the cross and the voice of the Messiah in anguish, "My God, My God, Why?" God was silent.

It is easy to lose hope in the silence.

Gordon Clinard writes that the darkest suffering of Job's experience was the silence of God. When God seems to be silent, it seems God does not care. If God had only answered Job's questions or intervened between him and his friends.

What then do we do when what we want, we cannot get? When what we need is not there? When what needs to change seems perpetual? What do we do when we are ready to move on but are caught between a rock and hard place?

The author of this ancient wisdom literature seems to tell his story to those who like Job. They struggle with the crises of faith brought on by prolonged bitter suffering. The author excellently uses poetry and prose that brings us to the edge of the suffering.

The story seems to be written by a sympathetic pastor. He is not writing as a detached theologian or philosopher. The book is intended for more than scholarly presentation and consultation. From it, we are to listen, love and learn.

This ancient wisdom talk gives us a Job who tells us his life has been put on hold. Ever been there?

You were minding your business—you were leaning with it, rockin' with it—then all of a sudden, everything changed. Do not adjust your set for you have entered the Twilight Zone. Hurricane Katrina, Hurricane Rita, downsizing, relocation, high gas prices, death, taxes, cancer, birth, divorce, separation, proposals, marriage and a miscarriage—Twilight Zone. Whether you wanted to or not, something happened and life was forever changed. Ask Leah. According to your rules of relationship, your expectation tells you that you expected God to do something but God is silent.

It is as if Job called heaven and he hears the following message:

"Your call is important to us. Either we are busy with other customers or are away from our divine desk or gone for the day. If you know your party's extension you may dial it now: for God, 1; the Son of God, 2; the Holy Spirit, 3; Mary, the mother of God, 4; Michael, the archangel, 5; guardian angels, 6; angels on assignment, 7; Peter, 8; John, 9; Paul, 10; Moses, 11. To reach our company directory, dial 12. At the tone, you may leave a detailed message or dial 0 for more options. Have a blessed day!"

Job says, "I looked all around and couldn't find God. I go forward. God is not there; backward, I cannot perceive him; on the left, I can't behold him. God hides himself on the right." (Job 23:8–9)

Job cannot see God and cannot hear God. He exists in that twilight space between what you had and what is on the way. Living in the gap is the silent place between what was and what is going to be.

In the midst of his challenges, the God Job expects to see, hear and act is silent. Job was still aware that God was present and knew his situation. Job declares, "He knows the way I take." (Job 23:10)

God knows the journey Job is taking and the path stretched out before him, the direction and the destination.

When we find ourselves in the gap of silence; we may not be able to see and hear our help but our help sees and hears us. Our help knows where we are headed and when it is going to be over. Tried and refined, like Job, we will come forth as pure gold!

After being tried, refined, worked with, and worked on—we will graduate with honors. There will be gaps of silence; we have all experienced it. There is no forward motion, no rear guard; there is a pause in the program, a work stoppage, a cease and desist order or a holding pattern before landing.

Do you think it is possible that God is watching to see if we will continue to follow God in spite of adverse circumstances which may surround us?

Job made the decision to keep following God. "My foot hath held his steps. His way I kept." (Job 23:11)

The hardest battles we will ever fight is the one when we are living in the gap of silence. When we are:

1. tempted to stray

2. tempted to leave

3. tempted to turn back

4. tempted to try another religion

5. tempted try another god

6. tempted to try another spirit

7. tempted to do your own thing

8. tempted to throw in the towel

9. tempted to curse somebody out

10. tempted to give up, give out, give away or just give 'em hell!

Job's wife tried to keep him from taking the necessary steps but Job was steadfast, and so must we be. Job wanted to obey God more than he wanted to do anything else. In the end, the story concludes that Job's life was better in the end than in the beginning.

Leah was in a tough place between her wedding night and the birth of her first son—the badge of honor for ancient women.

When we find ourselves living in the gap, we should do the next best thing. Do what you can where you are. Many times when you find yourself with tsunami events or caught in the eye of a hurricane with nothing but storms on every side, you can't go forward. You can't go backward,. Nor can you go to the right or the left.

Do the next best thing: get up, comb your hair, fix your face, call the insurance company, get an attorney, write the resignation letter, request a meeting, eat, exercise, jump for joy, shout hallelujah. Don't just sit there and wallow through your wait—do the next best thing!

God knows where you are and the path you must take. God will place in your path what you need for the road ahead.

Aunt Agony reminds us that a pause is not a permanent situation. Pause is a temporary inconvenience. "Girl, please don't buy anymore furniture for a temporary situation that will lead towards your permanent change."

Job never got an answer to his questions. And neither may we, when we approach the throne of grace. The pause is always with a purpose. Although you can't see it yet, the holding pattern just might be for your own good.

An air traffic controller will keep an aircraft in a holding pattern for a purpose, not just to pass the time away. It may be to wait until traffic dies down, to keep the plane from danger, to dump fuel, or because of crowded runways, storms in the area, tornado warnings, or a security alert. There is always a purpose to the pause. If you land too soon, you may find yourself in deeper danger.

Trust the divine traffic controller who knows where you are. The path you are to take will prepare you for your landing and it will be better in the end than the beginning.

God saw that Leah was hated. Leah had to find the courage to deal with difficult circumstances. Courage is often found in the heat of the battle. An anonymous writer once wrote, "Courage is fear that has said its prayers."

In 1992 when civil war broke out again, Katurah Cooper and her three young girls fled Liberia for the United States. Her husband, Jim Cooper, valiantly stayed behind. He tried to protect the family property and businesses. Rebel forces were fighting the government of then President Charles Taylor. Her family joined Payne Memorial AME Church in Baltimore when I served as senior pastor until my election to the episcopacy in 2000.

In the struggle for power, on three occasions Rev. Cooper's Liberian home was raided, bombed, ransacked and emptied of its contents. Yet, in 2001 during a tenuous ceasefire, she returned to rebuild her country and build a church—come hell or high water.

Dr. Lily Sanvee also had to find the courage to face her circumstances. She is the Medical Director and Chief Medical Officer for St. Joseph Catholic Hospital in Monrovia. Prior to her promotion, she had the responsibility of navigating the treacherous process to attend to wounded rebel fighters from different factions who now lay under the same roof. Fighters who espoused different ideologies and were from different tribal groups often shared the same ward and the same room. Tensions were high and tempers often flared.

"It was difficult dealing with them and their leaders at the same time I dealt with my own trauma and problems," she said. "Yet, I had to face the challenges and take care of them."

In 1992 and again in 2003, rebel fighters twice threatened the hospital where she worked. At one point, it became so dangerous that she was secretly taken in an ambulance to the ECOMOG (Economic Community

Monitoring Observer Group) military base. It was during a time when no one dared enter the streets. She was able to secure a promise from the base commander to send protection for the hospital.

When the rebel forces showed up at her hospital she was ready for the showdown. "I guess my male colleagues could not believe I could do that," she reflected.

Mrs. Margaret Malley's arm was cut off and her home was burned down during the civil conflict. She says she didn't feel sorry for herself and kept working for peace in her war torn country.

She was elected president of the Women of Liberia Mass Action for Peace and helped organize peace demonstrations.

"The fact that during the women sit-in action, there were times when I went to the sit-in fields even when bullets were flying overhead," she said. "The men did not take me seriously. They said I was not capable but I kept on because I considered this as serving God." This is courage to face your circumstance.

Today, the Honorable Neh Dukuly Tolbert serves Liberia as the Ambassador to the People's Republic of China. The mother of two sons, she considers raising her sons, her greatest accomplishment.

"The most challenging situation was when the *coup d'etat* that occurred in 1980. After the killing of President Tolbert and senior members of his family, I had to work with the military government that was in power," she said. "I had to worry about my survival and that of my two sons. Those were the most frightful moments of my life."

Counselor Lois Lewis Bruthus was captured along with 67 babies and adolescent mothers in Voinjama, Lofa County (rural Liberia). For five days in 1995, rebel forces held them without food and water. The threat of rape was constant. "We feared for our lives," she said

She returned from exile to become the President of the Association of Female Lawyers. She was determined to advocate the protection and rights of women and children. She passionately pursues a gender-harmony society in a conservative patriarchal country that in many instances sees women as assets or objects.

"The most relevant accomplishment is the restoration of self-esteem and self-worth to the 430 young adolescent mothers in the rural areas of Liberia," she stated. "Secondly, I serve as the focal point for the advocacy for the passage into law for the strengthening and expanding the Rape Bill."

She declared that gender bias was a global issue. Daily, Counselor Bruthus tried hard not to take prejudicial instances personally.

Her Excellency Ruth Sando Perry doesn't look like a woman who would survive living in dangerous conflict. A small gray-haired grandmother, she looks like a person who should be enjoying the sunset years of her life, surrounded by loving family and friends.

Time has slowed her steps but it cannot erase the footprints she made by negotiating a heroic cease-fire between six warring tribal factions and maintaining the cease-fire agreement among all six male rebel leaders during the civil war.

"On August 19, 1996, after I had retired for the night, I was summoned by the Nigerian President Sani Abacha. I was told to proceed immediately to the conference room filled with officials of the ECOWAS (Economic Community of West African States) and then taken to another room where the six military heads of the warring factions sat," said Her Excellency Perry in an interview.

There was no time to change from her nightclothes into appropriate attire. She was surprised at the invitation as she had not participated in the actual round table peace discussions that were held earlier in the day.

"These six men asked if I would consent to be the Head of State of Liberia and Chairwoman for the Council of State [which would consist of these six men]. I asked them why had they selected me? They said because 'you are the only one we can trust and because we see you as a mother, a reconciler and a neutral person.'"

Her Excellency Perry accepted the position to lead her country. Further, she was able to get the six male leaders to pledge to maintain a cease-fire and disarmament and conduct elections.

"While in my housedress, bedroom slippers and head wrap, I was escorted into the conference room where President Sani Abacha and the other African heads of state waited. They immediately stood and began addressing me as 'Your Excellency,'" she said. "My life changed forever from that moment even until now. The people of Liberia had democratically elected their first female president, the Honorable Ellen Johnson Sirleaf."

Job, the women of Liberia, and Leah all had to come to terms with God's silence and desperate situations. In Leah's case, God saw that Leah was hated and did something about it.

God saw her affliction and responded. The Creator was not a distant observer or passive participant. God became involved in a relationship that had sunk into the depths of deception.

God sees us right where we are. God knows the longitude and latitude of our physical and spiritual location. God knows us by situation and circumstance.

God never closes a door unless another is opened. The door to Jacob's heart was closed to Leah but God opened the door to Leah's womb. Leah had baby after baby. It would be through one of her children that Jesus Christ, the Messiah would come. Hated and rejected, God chose Leah's son Judah through which to bring God's only begotten Son, the One who would come to save God's people from their sins. The lineage of our Savior would not come from Rachel's two children or that of the other two women with whom Jacob slept.

Jacob loved Rachel, the woman who represented the glitter and gloss many men look for. She was his present but not the future. He hated Leah but she represented the future of the nation that would bare his name, Israel, and the coming Messiah.

Through her pain and suffering, Leah drew closer to God. She named her first son Reuben, which means "God has seen my suffering." Every time she looked at Reuben, every time she rocked, nursed, diapered or called his name, it reminded her that God had seen her misery and blessed her.

After Reuben's birth, another son named Simeon, meaning "one who hears," was born. When she gathered him in her arms it reminded her that God had heard her cry and had listened to her every prayer. After Simeon, Levi was born. This child's name means "attached," perhaps indicating that Leah hoped that this time Jacob would be attached to her.

Somewhere between Levi and the next child, something happened to Leah. Leah stopped focusing on Jacob. She stopped pursuing a dead issue and a love that wasn't going anywhere.

It seemed as though Leah had stopped investing herself in a relationship where there was no return. She stopped focusing on her problems, stopped focusing on her pain, and began to focus on God. When she began to focus on a power outside of herself, she began to praise God.

When the next child was born, Leah named him Judah. The name Judah means "Praise" and it also means "I will praise the Lord." The name of each of her eleven children was attached to her relationship with Jacob. Only Judah was attached to Jehovah. It would be through the child named, "I will praise the Lord" whom the Messianic child would be born.

After "Praise" was born, the Bible says that Leah stopped having babies. She stopped hating herself, she stopped hating her sister, and she stopped manipulating people around her. Leah stopped hurting, disintegrating, dying piece by piece or depending on people to bless her. She began to depend on God.

Praising God turns the lights back on into your life. Regardless of the difficulty, praise God! No matter how long the silence, praise God! When the one you love rejects you, praise God! When lovers lose their way, praise God! When it is hard to face your circumstances, praise God! When your courage loosens your faith, praise God! When you are put down by others, praise God! When you have been "messed over" on more than once occasion, praise God!

S.M.A.R.T. MOVES
(Spiritual Motivation for Action and Real Transformation)

Talking Points

1. Have you ever been rejected and discarded like a disposable product?

2. What are the unspoken rules in your family?

3. Have you ever pursued a dead-end relationship?

4. Leah, Job and the Liberian women found the courage to face desperate circumstances. After courage has said its prayers, what do you need to face?

5. Tonight, in your journal write your "coming of age" story.

The Word of Prayer

"I remember the awareness of the spirit of God that sought me out in my aloneness and gave me a sense of assurance that undercut my despair and confirmed my life with new courage and abiding hope." Amen. (Howard Thurman)

The Word of God

"We are troubled on every side, yet not distressed; we are perplexed, but not in despair; persecuted, but not forsaken; cast down, but not destroyed" (2 Corinthians 4:8–9)

Foreplay

Reintroduce your "self" to yourself today. Fall in love with you again. Remember what a great catch you are. Stop worrying about size, height, weight or "weak eyes." There is more to you than meets the eye. How you feel about yourself, positive or negative, will be communicated to those you care about.

Pillow Talk

You are the present and future in your relationship. Ask your spouse about his priorities and if you get a chance, share yours in the abbreviated version. You do want to get your rest!

Kiss and Tell

Don't kiss in your usual places. Find a different location other than the front or back door, bedroom or garage. Try the kitchen or the driveway. Make it short and very sweet. Tell him one unspoken rule so that he won't have to read your mind. And give him a chance to tell you his.

Kiss and Make Up

Oops! He does not like your unspoken rules and you are not partial to his. Do you want to have it your way, Mr. and Mrs. Burger King, or do you want a relationship?

Marital Madness

The two of you may have a different understanding about disclosure. One, usually the woman, may enjoy being open. The other, usually the man, may feel vulnerable. If you tell anyone what your spouse has shared with you (as long as it not illegal or dangerous to himself or others)—even with a best friend, he will feel betrayed. During an argument, if you ever threw what he told you in his face, it may be a long time before he will disclose his true feelings.

Singularity

Remember, the time and the place has a bearing upon a man's expectation of a relationship. You're either marriage material or a disposable girl.

SEVEN

GREEN-EYED MONSTER

And when Rachel saw that she bore
Jacob no children, Rachel envied her sister.
Genesis 30:1–13

Charm is deceptive and beauty is fleeting;
but a woman who fears the LORD is to be praised.
Proverbs 31:30

Envy is the art of counting the other fellow's
blessings instead of your own.
Harold Coffin

Deep in the heart of Texas, during a junior high school cheerleading competition, a mother wanted her daughter to have her moment in the spotlight. She wanted her daughter to have a shot at fame and glory on the football sidelines. Perhaps she would share in the excitement as she watched her daughter achieve what she wasn't allowed to do as a youngster.

When another girl was consistently chosen over her daughter, this mother believed that the mother of her daugther's competition was at fault. She allegedly solicited the help of her brother-in-law to kill the mother of her daughter's rival. Doing this heinous act would handicap her daughter's rival to compete. There was nothing in this woman's past to indicate that she could commit such an act.

Envy has been described as a frustrated desire that can become destructive. It is the painful awareness that someone is enjoying an advantage that you do not have. It is jealousy on steroids that combines discontent, resentment and desire.

Envy strikes out at the envied but ends up hurting itself. It desires to covet what someone else has, believing that another has gained something that rightfully belongs to them.

Philosopher John Rawls distinguishes between jealousy and envy. He notes that jealousy is the desire to keep what you already have while envy is the desire to get what you do not have.

Another writer contends that envy will either motivate you toward excelling or wishing ill will towards a rival. You will either rise to the occasion or sink below the murky green waters of envy. The sinking feeling is translated when you wish for another's failure and your success. You might want to see that person broke, disfigured, unemployed or divorced —as you covet another's possessions. On one hand, you are glad that your friend has a nice car. On the other hand, you want the car and if you can't have it, you want to destroy it.

Welcome to the land of Rachel the beautiful, Leah the unwanted, and Jacob the deceiver deceived. Envy and jealousy were a part of the matrix of emotions that caused tensions in their household.

Perhaps, unloved Leah was jealous of her sister and had feelings of resentment towards her. Leah had Jacob's body but not his head or heart. Rachel had his heart but could not conceive with him.

Rachel was in an unfamiliar position. She was always adored and appreciated. She was the younger beauty to her older weak eyed sister. Rachel was envious of her sister's proclivity to procreate—a celebrated position in ancient Hebrew culture.

Genesta was convinced that Raul loved her in spite of his engagement to Penelope. After all, he was Genesta's baby's daddy. He visited her at least twice a week to see his son and invariably they would end up in bed together.

Raul told Genesta that she was like a bad habit. She felt good to Raul but she wasn't good enough to be a part of his future. He enjoyed her expertise in bed but he always wondered with whom she had garnered all of her experience. He didn't have to worry about such things with Penelope. His fiancé wouldn't let him do to her what he was able to do to Genesta. He had done his "background check" on Penelope. She had a clean reputation. Genesta, on the other hand, was well known in the neighborhood.

Once Raul married Penelope, he secretly planned to file for custody of his son. He knew that if it wasn't him in bed with Genesta, it would be someone else between her sheets. He didn't want his son to grow up in that kind of environment.

Genesta envied Penelope. She believed that Raul was rightfully hers and this "Jackie-come-lately" was messing up everything.

Genesta decided to confront Penelope at work. She was going to warn her to stay away from her baby's daddy. So, she gathered all the baby's photographs along with intimate pictures she had taken with Raul. Genesta had planned to scare and embarrass Penelope in front of her co-workers.

Like the Greek mythology goddess Hera, who went into a jealous raged over Zeus's lovers, Genesta flew into a rage of legendary proportions. She cried, screamed and cursed Penelope. She pinned Penelope into a corner and reduced her to a sniffling puddle. The police were called. They put an end to Genesta's tirade.

Raul couldn't convince Penelope that Genesta's strategy was to drive a wedge between them. Genesta's plan worked. The wedding was cancelled.

Genesta was a regular client at our Power Center when I pastored Oak Street AME Church in East Baltimore. One afternoon following our Wednesday luncheon service,, she told me the story. She confessed that now that she had gotten Penelope out of the picture, she really didn't want Raul anymore.

It is amazing the numbers of time we want someone simply because someone else has him or her. You weren't interested in the man until he was on somebody else's arm. The ice cream didn't tempt you until the person next to you started devouring it. The promotion was not appealing until your office rival applied for the job. The car had no allure for you until your neighbor bought one. The woman was not on your hit list until your buddy started dating her. You weren't interested in having children until your cousin started giving birth to stair steps.

Be honest. How many times have you looked at someone who belonged to someone else, fantasized about dating him, calling him, and even marrying him? It could be a spouse of a family member, best friend, next door neighbor or a married pastor. All of these thoughts can lead to trouble.

Aunt Agony says it's called "lusting in the heart." "Get your own life and leave others alone!"

True or false: you purchased a fur coat because she got a new fur coat; you bought a bigger diamond because she had a big diamond; you bought a St. John knit suit because she bought a St. John knit suit; you collect silk flowers because she collects silk flowers; you bought Baby Phat jeans because if she could look good in Baby Phat jeans so could you; you purchased a Bentley because she purchased a Bentley. It almost sounds like the song, "anything you can do I can do better, I can do anything better than you!"

Sandy confessed she had no interest in having children right after she married Lawrence. Suddenly, during her first year of marriage, Sandy had this obsession that she had to get pregnant.

Years later, she realized that the impetus for her desire to get pregnant was because her two best friends were pregnant and had baby showers. She felt left out. She wanted to enjoy the attention that was showered upon them. It is called envy—longing to possess something achieved by someone else.

Susan Shapiro Barash writes that most American women have their identities wrapped up in their perception of other women. In *Tripping the Prom Queen: The Truth about Women and Rivalry*, Barash says that for a variety of reasons, we view who we are by comparing ourselves to sisters, friends, mothers, co-workers and peers. We do not see ourselves separate from others or with separate destinies. We do not rise or fall on our own merits. Some of us do so only if we measure ourselves to those closest to us or to powerful women we know or see in the media.

There seems to be a great fascination about how hungry our culture is to watch women compete on television programs like *America's Next Top Model*, *The Bachelor* or *The Apprentice*. There is also a greater fascination with women who fail versus women of power who succeed.

Anna Nicole Smith received more media print and air time in the death of her son and her subsequent death than she received over her career as a *Playboy* Model or movie star. Martha Stewart's star rose high after her legal woes and according to Barash, so did Hillary Clinton's after the embarrassment of President Clinton and Monica Lewinsky. Hillary Clinton was the wronged wife.

Vicariously, we cannot compete with women like Stewart, Clinton, Smith, Beyonce, Angelina Joli, Mary J. Blige, Oprah Winfrey and others. We enjoy them competing with each other and, says Barash, we enjoy seeing them fail. We gain when other women lose.

Aunt Agony says, "Get a life!"

It is a tough indictment on how women treat each other. This is not to say that men do not experience the intense emotional feelings of envy and jealousy. They do too!

In my sanctified imagination, Rachel was accustomed to success. Her power potion was her beauty. It probably wasn't a surprise to her that Jacob could not take his eyes off of her when they first met at the well.

Rachel probably enjoyed the attention that her beauty garnered. She had enjoyed the attention of men wherever she went.

We all know modern-day Rachels. Everyone else spends time and money on expensive hair treatments, Rachel shook her tresses and it just fell into place with ease. Others have to carefully select a wardrobe that hides hips, thighs, love handles, and stomachs. Not Rachel.

Other women have to be creative with makeup to conceal blemishes. Not Rachel. Exorbitant funds were spent with orthodontists to fix and rearrange teeth. Not Rachel.

The Rachels of this world always seem to float between a size 8 and 10 and their feet look great in any style shoe. She's probably organized, funny, witty and articulate. And she can field compliments because she expects them.

The Leahs of this world look into a mirror and see only the negatives—like pimples, rough skin, and blotches. She cringes inside when a compliment is given. Surely the giver is being solicitous or mistaken. Silent jealousy diminishes her strengths and self-confidence, sending her to a plastic surgeon for Botox, liposuction, tummy tuck, nose job, or face lift. She might even pay for a membership at a gym.

All Rachel has to do is show up. She could walk across the room and have every man's eyes trailing behind her. When she walked, men signed. When she batted her eyes, men just die. When she stood up to straighten out her clothes, men would break out into a cold sweat.

When men went to sleep, they dreamed of Rachel. In her community, when a little boy was asked whom he wanted to marry when he grew up, it would be Rachel. Rachel walked with confidence. She lived with confidence that in the pecking order of women's relationships, she was at the top.

It seemed Jacob had to do what a man had to do in his cultural set-up. In order to have Rachel, he had to work 14 long years and also take on a second wife. Leah was just an added responsibility. She was his, by deception, not by desire. Jacob, however, had no problem sleeping with Leah enough times to have sired four children in quick succession.

Rachel reacted with envy. The New Revised Standard version says that Rachel was jealous of her sister, because her sister was having babies.

Sandy felt left out. She felt her friends had somehow gained an advantage over her by having children. In Rachel's case, Leah did have an advantage.

The unloved Leah usurped her sister's most valuable player status by giving Jacob sons. Sons were especially valued in this ancient Hebrew culture. Sons would pass on the family name, manage the family business, and provide protection and perhaps stability to the extended family, including parents as they advanced in years. Sons were ranked by age. Therefore, the eldest had the most power and could act in the father's absence.

In this polygamous community, children were born to different women but were connected by the father, who oftentimes was a "remote" father. An example of remote parenting would be the gap between David and his son Absalom. The distance was such that the son tried to displace his father from the throne. (2 Samuel 15:14; 17:2–4)

Rivalry, envy, jealousy and bitterness were often a by-product of such relationships. Jacob had two women to satisfy; two attitudes to endure; and two personalities to get to know. He had to support two different women who lived in the same place, at the same time. Marriage is challenging enough with one spouse. It is difficult enough to live with one family let alone blended relationships.

Penninah bore sons for Elkanah but Hannah did not. No amount of expressions of love would sooth her. She wasn't content until God opened her womb and Samuel was born.

Sarah was old and barren when the promise of an heir was given to her. Unwilling to wait on God, she manipulated the promise by giving her servant Hagar to lie with her husband and produce an heir child.

Women may have been secluded and silent in this culture, yet they were able to exert power and influence power. Rebecca favored Jacob over Esau. She strategically planned for her husband to bless her favorite son, the younger son, rather than the elder twin. Sarah, who convinced Abraham to have a sexual relationship with Hagar, also convinced him to expel her and her son from the family after she bore Isaac. Rachel and Leah forced the procreation issue beyond their marriage tent to include two others, Bilhah and Zilpah.

Rachel was envious of her sister's blessing. She wanted to participate in a baby contest to see who would give Jacob the most. Her equipment may have been beautiful but it was unable to produce an heir.

Rachel was hot! She was angry, bitter and envious. She had been accustomed to winning. She had been accustomed to having the "upper hand." She was used to getting all the attention. The baby showers, however, were not being held for her. They were held for Leah. Gifts were coming for Leah's children. Accolades and praises were directed at Leah the fruitful, leaving Rachel the barren out.

Her sister had achieved an envious status. Jacob's love did not appease her, just like Elkanah's love didn't sooth Hannah.

Rachel's envy turned destructive when she boldly confronted Jacob. "Give me children or I will die." (Genesis 30:1) She demanded performance and production from her husband. It was procreation on demand. Rachel's cutting criticism revealed the depth of her hurt and anguish.

"Give me what I want and give it to me now! Give me the same thing you gave to Leah. I have heard you in the other tent night after night, laughing with Leah all night. Laugh with me like that," Rachel could have said.

"I see you smiling at her across the table in the morning. I see you choose her tent over mine in the evening. You spend too much time at her tent and not enough time in mine. I am tired of hearing what baby Reuben did today. I do not want to hear how Simeon is cutting a new tooth. I am tired of hearing how you will be glad when Levi is old enough to go help you tend the sheep. Give me what I want now."

Criticism turned to contempt. Contempt turned into bitterness. Hebrews 12:15, however, reminds us that no root of bitterness springs up and causes trouble, for by it many will be devoured. Every time anger turns into bitterness and finds a home in one's heart, it will spring up and cause trouble.

Oftentimes, we do not know what to do with our bitterness. We try to suppress it. We bite our tongues. We hold our peace. We clinch our jaws and grind our teeth. Then one day, bitterness erupts to confront a rival, plan a murder for hire or make unreasonable demands. It shouts, demands, chastises, and castrates—just like Rachel was trying to do to Jacob. Rachel questioned his masculinity. She questioned his manhood.

Carmella was Jack's second wife. The children from the first marriage were teenagers but Carmella wanted a baby. Jack was reluctant because he had already endured the diaper and babysitter period. He loved his children but also loved a quiet house with only two adults.

He didn't mind the regular visits from his children that included loud music, noise, emptying the refrigerator and losing control of the remote. He was happy to see them come and he was happy to see them go.

One night in our Married Couples Ministry meeting, Carmella admitted that she was jealous. She felt that there was still a bond between Jack and his first wife because of their kids. A bond she knew they could have if they had a child together.

Besides, she wasn't their mother and never would be. His kids resented her and resisted anything that looked like discipline. She felt she was forced into the role of the wicked stepmother, with Jack the knight in shining armor role. Jack felt he had only a weekend with his children. He didn't want to spend the time with a lot of do's and don'ts.

It got to the point that the mere mention of Jack's first wife sent Carmella into a ranting rage. She couldn't shake the feeling. It was just unfair that Jack didn't want kids with her. Her jealousy turned into "What does she have that I don't have?" "What's the matter with me?" or "What's the matter with you?"

With the help of a marriage counselor, Jack and Carmella were able to work through their blended family issues. They learned that stepfamilies do not function like other families but have their own unique set of behaviors and dynamics. Jack learned that he had to establish house rules and boundaries for the teens. Carmella learned that even though she would never be their mother, she could have a positive influence upon them.

They established "knights of the round table" discussions, in which at the beginning of a visitation each member of the family could share where they were in their world of school, work and other activities.

Problems such as conflicting loyalties, the "play daddy" weekend syndrome and expectations were discussed.

Carmella still wants to have a child of her own. She was tempted to slip and get pregnant but she would rather have a baby with Jack's cooperation than without it.

For that, Aunt Agony said Carmella should get the Nobel Stepmother Peace Prize!

Jacob became angry with Rachel. He responded, "Am I in the place of God, who has kept you from having children? (Genesis 30:2)

Rachel preferred death over a childless existence. It didn't matter whether she was loved more than Leah. She had financial security. She had tents and servants of her own. She occupied a special place in her husband's heart.

Yet, she was preoccupied with what was happening in other women's tents than in her own. Every baby born was a blow to Rachel's self-esteem and to her womanhood. She was wounded and she wanted to strike back.

She had a "greener grass" problem. The grass is always greener in the other woman's tent or bedroom. Rachel was in such a hurry to add children to the equation that her envy was driving a wedge between her and Jacob—similar to what was happening between Carmella and Jack.

Isaiah 54:10 indicates that God's loving kindness would never be removed from you. Human love often depends upon the other person's willingness to return love. Divine love is anchored in a relationship with God who can't help but love us. His unfailing was demonstrated on the cross, for while we were yet sinners, Jesus died for us.

Oftentimes, we ask for more than a person can possibly give. It is only when we yield ourselves to Jesus Christ that real satisfaction comes.

Marriage means that we have a partner of a lifetime. It is a sacred covenant blessed by God. It is more than a contract for a specific period of time. It is a relationship built on mutuality whose trinity is he, she and God.

Sometimes a spouse will be there for you and sometimes he won't. Sometimes he will do right and sometimes he won't. Marriage is filled with both joy and sorrow. It can be unique, beautiful, exotic, and mundane. It is filled with the ordinary and the tedious. It is a rites of passage from youth to mature adulthood. It is growing old together, accepting the changes that come with growth, maturity and experience. Some things will get better and other things may be troublesome. God gives us the gift to serve and support each other.

When we get in trouble, however, we look to our committed covenant companion to be there to help. Our partners check our foreheads when we are feverish and they cry with us when our parents are lowered into the grave. They tell us we look nice even on a bad hair day.

Rachel wanted Jacob to give her children but it wasn't Jacob's call. It doesn't matter how many sperms and eggs are cultivated in a laboratory, it is still God who grants life. The Lord gives and the Lord takes away. The Creator and giver of life is the one who grants the fruit of the womb.

Waiting for her fruitfulness was an excruciating time in Rachel's life. She had the right man and made all of the right moves. She had followed the instructions in the direction manual. However, she was still empty and barren.

When you are frustrated in the waiting process, you often begin to make demands on those around you. We become upset. We bite our fingernails. We lose our hair. We add another wrinkle. We eat too much. We sleep too little or we do not eat at all. Like Rachel, we tend to get so impatient that we live with unrealistic expectations.

Rachel fought back the only way she knew how—by manipulating and controlling the people in her life. Her solution to the problem was to use her servant Bilhah as a surrogate mother. She offered Bilhah to Jacob. Rachel would vicariously give birth through her servant.

I have often wondered about the thoughts of female servants who were used as surrogate mothers and/or concubines for the male head of the family. Bilhah may not have wanted to have children or she might not have wanted Jacob to father her children. She could have had eyes on another man in the community. This may have been culturally correct but it sure rearranges a woman's agenda.

Bilhah was forced into an intimate relationship. She bore him a son. Rachel responded that God had vindicated her and listened to her pleas and given her a son. She named him Daniel, meaning "vindicated."

The servant became pregnant a second time. Rachel responded that she had a great struggle with her sister and won. She named the son Naphtali, meaning "my struggle."

The baby contest was now in full force with Leah joining in the fray. Leah, now unable to have children, takes her maidservant Zilpah and gave her to Jacob as a wife. Zilpah bears Jacob a son. She names him Gad, meaning "good fortune." The second son was soon born and Leah named him Asher, meaning "happy."

This sounds like a baby contest that had become a baby war. The warfare was now escalating. It not only disrupted the original three lives, but it was now affecting five different adults. Five adults had been pulled into a marital quagmire—not counting the eight children borne to three different mothers.

If there were a psychiatrist present, he or she would have been able to tell them what constituted a truly dysfunctional family. There was neglect, sexual merry go rounds, misplaced priorities, manipulation and greed.

Jacob was reduced to a mere sexual satisfaction. He was no longer a man but a machine to perform and produce with whatever woman was given him. All day Jacob worked the fields, and all night he worked in the tents. Jacob did not complain, he just followed directions because of Rachel's jealousy!

If we harbor envy and selfish ambition in our hearts, we should not boast or deny the truth. (James 3:14) Carmella was able to confess her envy in a group setting and later in counseling. Genesta was out of control, unable to admit her deep-seated envy until she inflicted serious harm. We are also encouraged not to think more highly of ourselves than we should. We should think soberly.

Aunt Agony says, "That it is easier said than done. Hon, when you wear green-eyed contact lenses everywhere you look, you will want what you don't have."

Every now and then life will throw you a green-eyed curve. It's like a good change-up pitcher in a baseball game. The pitcher lulls a batter into thinking he is only going to throw a fastball but instead sends a slider or one that will slightly drop across the plate.

A good change-up pitcher knows how to feed a pattern of pitches to the batter. Just when the batter is convinced that the next pitch is going to be a fastball, the pitcher throws a curveball. It catches the batter off guard. The next thing he knows is that he is on the way back to the dugout wondering what happened.

Life has a way of moving along in predictable patterns. It can lead you along until you can almost predict what will come next. Then before you know, it snows on Easter, there are springlike temperatures in the Northeast in December, there are wildfires in California, a luxury cruise ship sinks, a tsunami hits the Pacific Rim and kills thousands, or you are hit in the gut with a nasty mixture of envy, jealousy, resentment and bitterness.

You are having a hard time living beyond your emotional tsunamis just as thousands are trying to survive the damage left by the levees that broke in Louisiana.

This Molotov cocktail of emotions leaves you stranded. You become vulnerable to the cousins of envy, which include spite, begrudging and discontent.

Psalm 34 provides a recipe for serenity. It belongs to a group of ten psalms that deal generally with being happy. The psalm helps the singers shape the understanding of happiness. It is not the same as pleasure or bliss. Happiness is shown to be a state in which the definition of a Godly life is one of moral restraint lived with Joy.

One commentator suggests that those who are blessed live without the worry that is caused by guilt. Why? Because they know their sins have been forgiven. Nations are blessed when they find their security in God. Those who are faithful to God, those who are innocent before their accusers, those who help others, and those who fear God are blessed.

The blessedness does not mean that this is a life without anguish, pain or suffering. The righteous are not immune from distress. As Jesus says, "In this world you face persecution. But take courage; I have conquered the world!" (John 16:33)

Psalm 34 has been characterized as a teaching psalm because all but one verse begins with a different letter of the Hebrew alphabet. The alphabetical order may have been a tool to help students learn easier or faster. If they can memorize it, they can believe it. If they believe it, they can do it.

The psalm begins with the first part of the recipe. This is the intense repetitive habit of praising God. "I will bless the Lord at all times. His praise shall continually be in my mouth." Leah had reached that moment with the birth of Judah but Rachel had yet to arrive.

Blessing God means we should praise God in the good times, in the challenging times, and in stressful times. This has to be honest to goodness praise. It shouldn't be praise to impress people or to manipulate a congregation. It should be the type of praise that gives external affirmation to God—not only as a demonstration to show others you know how to publicly praise God. Praising God is infectious when it flows from the heart of the worshipper through the lips of the prayers to the ear of God. It soars to join the continuous chorus of the Seraphim and Cherubim.

When wading through the destructive murky mixture of envy and jealousy, praising God becomes an act of will. It is insistent praise such as: I will bless the Lord in spite of what I feel and because of what is happening. I will bless the Lord when all is well with my soul and when life throws me a curve!

The psalmist said he will bless the Lord all the time and issues an invitation for others to do the same. Come magnify the Lord with me and let us exalt His name together.

The historical background of the psalm is located in 1 Samuel 21:10–15 where David pretends insanity to escape from the Philistine ruler. He testifies about being delivered by God and invites others to taste and see that the Lord is good.

God's love for him is a humbling experience. God will allow him to stick out his tongue to taste before committing. There is the assurance of the presence of God to the poor, to stricken humanity, and to those who have felt the brunt of life's curveballs.

It concludes by offering hope. The Lord is near the brokenhearted and saves the crushed in spirit. Many are the affliction of the righteous but God delivers then out of them all.

This psalm is an encouragement to help us when we want what we can't have. It also offers hope to keep us from destroying what we do have.

Maurice Lamm expounds on hope in his book *The Power of Hope*. He writes that hope is a three-story house.

The first story is incremental hope. This is sensible hope that is characterized by a hope that will not bite off more than it can chew. It is one-step-at-a-time hope that moves gradually towards a single solution

Trevor was a wonderful pastor with a sweet disposition. He was loved by his members with the exception of an elderly couple. They had nothing positive to say to family, friends or other members about him. It seemed like one of them would purposely make the final comment at every church meeting—a comment that would cut deep into Trevor's heart.

Trevor was advised by the other members to take the elderly gentleman off the Steward Board because he was not helping but hurting the ministry. Trevor refused.

He wrote "thinking of you notes" to the couple on a regular basis. He sent cards to them on holidays and checked on them in inclement weather. He made an effort to be complimentary to each of them. He had to bite his tongue on more than one occasion when the couple was rude.

Step by step, Trevor kept working on them until they called and made an appointment. In the young pastor's office, the couple admitted they were wrong to be angry with him. Their son had committed suicide. The pastor reminded them so much of their son that all the anger they felt over his death was transferred to him. They were jealous because the church had a pastor but they did not have their son. After tears and prayer, they reached a resolution.

Lamm says we get into trouble when we try to do something all at once, rather than taking small steps. Incremental hope works every day to take the basic steps to solve a problem. It is like the one-day-at-a-time philosophy of the various twelve step programs. Survival, resolution, reconciliation, and reunions are doing what you can, where you are, and with what you have to work with until you can do better. Apologize to someone even if your envy struck out at someone. Pray and ask God to help you celebrate another's success. Console someone rather than rejoice in the person's failure. Admit to yourself that you were secretly wishing a particular person would fall apart, break up, cave in, and be ruined. Go ahead and write a letter, make a telephone call and clean up the mess your jealousy created.

Sometimes all you can do is remember that God is near.

The second story of the three-story house is high hopes. This is the hope that is distant. Rather than a step-by-step hope, it is more like a leaps-and-bounds type of hope.

For many years, I worked in broadcasting. One day my colleagues and I were taking a break from our responsibilities between our air shifts to talk about the future. One of us wanted to take a few classes at a school of communications, and then one day become a program director, operations manager, or general manager. Another wanted to own several radio stations. The first desire was an incremental step-by-step hope. The other was high hopes that reached beyond the steps to the ultimate goal.

The third story is ecstatic hope. This is where I live everyday. This is hope that cannot be justified. It is a supernatural hope that is encouraged by the Holy Spirit. It is a radical hope based on the word of God.

It is an unreasonable hope that says, like Job, "even though he slays me, yet will I trust him." It is a hope that says, like the psalmist, "weeping endures for a night but I know that joy will come in the morning." It is the hope testimony of Mary, "for nothing is impossible with God."

There is a story that is often told about poor people who lived in New York City in the early 20th century. They lived in squalor in a run-down tenement. Cultures and races were crunched layer upon layer in horrific conditions. An author wrote a book about the tenement residents. He concluded, "They kept their vision even in the dark."

This is an outrageous hope that miraculously makes sense when life throws you a curve: barren womb; family intrigue; promotions passing you by; blessings going everywhere but to your house; the one you want is on someone else's arm; or you believe others have some advantage that you somehow deserve.

Dwell on Psalm 34. Put together the recipe for serenity: The continuous habitual praise to Almighty God for God's mighty acts. Praise God for God's righteousness. Praise God for deliverance. Praise God for being blessed with every spiritual blessing. Praise God for what God has already done for you and what you already possess. Apply the right hope to the appropriate situation to help you through seasons of envy and jealousy.

Remember Rachel and Leah. The Lord is near, hope thou in God.

S.M.A.R.T. MOVES
(Spiritual Motivation for Action and Real Transformation)

Talking Points

1. Have you ever celebrated the failure of another woman?

2. Has envy or jealousy ruined one of your relationships?

3. Why do think some women identify more with a woman's failure rather than her success?

4. What are some of the do's and don'ts for blended families?

5. Using Maurice Lamm's description of the three stories of hope, plot your own response to a difficult situation.

6. Using Psalm 34, write your own recipe for serenity in 21st century language.

7. Do you give and receive compliments well?

The Word of Prayer

God, forgive my envious thoughts and my critical spirit that celebrates failure and criticizes success. Help me to see the unique gifts you have bestowed upon me. Help me to accentuate my strengths and make appropriate improvement on my weaknesses.

The Word of God

"Let us live honorably as in the day, not in reveling and drunkenness, not in debauchery and licentiousness, not in quarreling and jealousy. Instead, put on the Lord Jesus Christ, and make no provision for the flesh, to gratify its desires." (Romans 13:13–14)

Foreplay

This morning, along with your spouse, make a conscious effort to bless God at all times.

Pillow Talk

With your spouse, share the joy over someone's recent achievements, successes or accomplishments.

Kiss and Tell

Remember to kiss like you mean it. Now disconnect and go to a mirror and tell yourself only good things.

Kiss and Makeup

Sometimes jealousy and envy can motivate a person to change and make improvements. Sometimes it can be destructive. If your jealousy has got the best of you, say you are sorry and move on.

Marital Madness

It is madness to allow your jealousy and envy to keep your spouse away from activities and friends. Your nervousness, your selfishness, and your perception of those around you is not your spouse's problem. Share your troubles rather then striking out in ways that can destroy your relationship.

Singularity

Those who are single can also get the green-eyed jealousy syndrome against those who are married. The same is true for those who are married with children and those who are not.

Let the perfect love of God cast out the green-eyed monster in your life. Remember, envy will make you believe that the grass is always greener in the other woman's bedroom.

EIGHT

WRESTLING AGAINST FLESH AND BLOOD

And Rachel said,
"With great wrestling have I wrestled with
my sister and I have prevailed."

Genesis 30:8

Some days we're on top of the world.
Other days we feel fragile. Whatever we go through,
we might as well do it in style,
so put on your pearls girl!

Lulu Guiness

Surviving is important. Thriving is elegant.

Maya Angelou

A few years ago, Stan and I visited his family in Florida. He is the seventh and last child born to Olive and Luke McKenzie. More than a decade in age separates him and his oldest brother.

While enjoying an afternoon of food and fun, I watched the three brothers closest in age participate in a rousing dance—each vying for everyone's attention. It was amazing. One used jokes while the other told stories and the third trumped the other two by emerging from the kitchen with a fresh batch of fried conch fritters. Laughter filled the room.

Later that evening, I teased Stan about how he and his brothers—as old as they were—vied for attention. "Nonsense!" was his response. "We do that all the time. We're just having fun. It's harmless."

"True enough for you," was my reply.

In many families, sibling rivalry is not fun and games. It causes conflict, pain and negative circumstances that can continue into adult life.

In Rachel and Leah's family, it wasn't harmless or fun. They were unable to put away childish things. One sister could have been favored by one or both parents. This sibling rivalry manifested itself in adulthood as the two sisters wrestled to obtain Jacob's attention and affection. Their actions were very much like children who wrestle for the love and attention of a parent.

Ariel and Adrienne are twins who were born while their mother was in prison. During labor, their mother died. For a period of time, no one, not even their father, came forward to claim them. Eventually their maternal grandmother agreed to raise them. With limited resources, she was able to provide them with food, clothes and shelter. Occasionally, they would receive money for a movie or a summer outing. Most of the time, however, if the event wasn't free, they couldn't go.

Fashionable designer clothes, such as Baby Phat and J Lo, and designer shoes were not a part of their wardrobe. Neither were fashionable "hoodies" or expensive jeans from expensive boutiques.

Their grandmother focused on their education. Immediately after school and before play time or chores, she made the girls do their homework. She pushed them to excel so that they would be eligible for a scholarship to a good university or college.

The girls competed vigorously for their grandmother's attention. The one with the highest grades was rewarded. The one who came in first place was lavished with attention. The one who finished her chores first and the best, received attention that the other craved.

Adrienne played the role of the "good girl." She did a better job competing and winning her grandmother's favor. On the other hand, Ariel rejected the "nice girl" persona. She felt nice girls finished last. She wore her clothes a little too tight and she was always making off-color comments.

Ariel learned that she didn't have to push too hard to win her share of affection. All she needed to do was to make Adrienne look bad. In turn, she would look good.

When Adrienne caught Ariel in one of the many lies she often told her grandmother, it was Adrienne who was chastised. Ariel played on her grandmother's sympathy and often her indiscretions were overlooked or ignored. Adrienne learned how to be a victim while her sister learned how to win her way into her grandmother's heart.

In their senior year of high school, both girls were eligible to apply for a scholarship. Adrienne did not get a scholarship but Ariel did. She won it with a little backroom manipulation. It was the same thing she did at home—she made herself look good by making her sister look bad. Ariel went off to school while Adrienne worked and attended the local community college.

While in school, Ariel was supported by her grandmother's retirement and whatever money her sister could send. Adrienne was proud that her sister was attending a big time, out of state university. Secretly, however, she wished she could take her sister's place.

In Ariel's junior year, her grandmother died and she became a financial strain on Adrienne. Fortunately, Adrienne had graduated from her two-year community college and rather than continue her education at a four-year college, she worked to help Ariel finish school. Adrienne stepped into the role of the supportive caretaker, determined not to abort her goal to help her sister stay in school and her grandmother's dream.

Ariel was always writing home for more money. Adrienne didn't realize how expensive books in Ariel's field of study were or how expensive it was to live on campus. What Adrienne really didn't know was that Ariel had a full scholarship. She wrote home for more money so that she could eat out, buy the latest fashions, CDs, and other gadgets.

Ariel had a job and a credit card. She was living a sweet life while Adrienne lived in her grandmother's tiny apartment. In an effort to support her sister, Ariel often went without heat in the winter and air conditioning in the summer.

When it was time for Ariel to graduate, Adrienne made plans to surprise Ariel by attending her graduation. It would be her first trip out of the state and her first bus trip anywhere.

When Adrienne arrived at her sister's college, she went directly to the address where she had sent Ariel's monthly checks. Upon arriving at the address, she discovered that Ariel was no longer living in the dormitory but in a condominium off campus. According to people who knew her, Ariel was living with a man twice her age in a huge beautifully furnished three bedroom condominium.

Adrienne couldn't believe her ears. She had sacrificed, scraped, and saved every penny to help support Ariel because she wanted her to succeed. It never occurred to Adrienne that Ariel would still be up to her old tricks.

Ariel really didn't need the money but she asked for it anyway. She couldn't care less about the hardship she created for her sister. Their sibling rivalry had continued into adulthood.

Ariel felt she was entitled to her sister's support because her grandmother had promised that she would send her money while she was in school. Even though her grandmother had died, Ariel felt it was now her sister's responsibility to support her.

"You owe me!" was Ariel's response when she saw her sister standing at her front door. Adrienne was speechless. If looks could kill, her twin sister would have died on the spot.

Adrienne was horrified that her sister would do this to her. She was so shocked that all she wanted to do was slink back to her tiny apartment. After so many years, once again she felt victimized.

Adrienne listened to her sister talk about her graduation plans and the good job she had been offered. More importantly, she met Richard, Ariel's boyfriend, who according to Ariel wanted to marry her. Richard lavished Ariel with gifts and paid for her clothes, including the condo. Ariel even had her driver's license and the use of Richard's car. "Be happy for me," she said to Adrienne.

After being introduced to Richard, it suddenly occurred to Adrienne that Ariel owed *her*. She began to plot a way to take her sister's place. This time she would not lose. She was not going back to the tiny apartment she grew up in. This time, she was playing for keeps. The prize was not a scholarship but a new lifestyle.

The spirit of competition exhibited by Rachel and Leah during their childhood was alive and well in their adult years. It could have been a result of favoritism shown to one, or the expectations for success were higher for one sister and not the other.

The roles of victim and victor swung back and forth between Rachel and Leah. Rachel had to contend with her sister and now had the upper hand. Two children were born to Rachel's handmaid. The victim was now the victor!

Just as the tables had turned in her favor, they would swing back in Leah's direction. Leah decided to give her handmaid Zilpah to Jacob to wed. The score was made even when her servant gave birth to two more sons.

Conscious or unconscious, some people recreate their childhood in adulthood. Like Ariel and Adrienne, it is either with the same cast of characters or, like Rachel and Leah, with a new group. This time, they may live with the hope that they could fix their broken past and create a different ending.

Ariel and Adrienne always seemed to be attracted to older men. In reality, they looked for a parent to replace the one they never had. Years later and after several failed marriages, they were able to admit they were really looking for a "replacement parent."

They played the recurring role of the little girl seeking the affection and attention of the parent. It worked then and they expected to be successful at the game.

Richard left Ariel. He was tired of the relationship with the twins and tired of playing "sugar daddy." In the beginning, it was a great ego booster to have two very young women competing for his attention. They made him feel young again. But, after a while, the fun waned.

Richard got very tired of the pouting, whining and temper tantrums when one of them didn't get their way. He had already raised his children and he was not looking to raise two more. Richard wanted companionship but he was looking for it in the wrong direction.

"Better to live in a desert than with a quarrelsome and ill-tempered wife." (Proverbs 21:19) Aunt Agony says the same could be said about living with ill-tempered husbands!

Sometimes the dynamics of childhood are recreated in adulthood so that a wrong can be avenged. The spouse pays the debt for the sins of the parent(s) or lack thereof. Adrienne and Ariel did to each husband what they had wanted to do to their mother who died in prison and the father they never knew.

In other situations, people relive their childhood hoping to heal or hoping that the story will have a different ending. Your past is what you know. When familial situations do not reflect what you know, even when negative, it can produce anxiety. An unconscious urge kicks in, and you become who you use to be.

One day, Cassie woke up and realized that she was yelling at her children in the same manner that her parents had yelled at her. She hurled the same labels. One son was called "stupid" and the other her "brilliant baby." Stupid was also called Lazy, Dopey or Bowfinger, after an Eddie Murphy character. Brilliant Baby was praised as a cute, smart little man who one day would make his mamma proud. The comparisons served to create tension and rivalry between her sons. Her name calling pales in respect to what they call each other now that they are adults.

Carrie tried to restrain herself but she said she couldn't help it. It is like the author of Romans expressed: she did what she didn't want to do, and what she wanted to do didn't happen. (Romans 7:14–20)

Matthew's father was physically present but emotionally absent when he was growing up. A few years ago, he was promoted to the vice presidency of a large manufacturing company. The position came with great pay but it also came with greater responsibility that consumed 12 to 16 hours of his day.

Although he wanted the closeness of his wife and son, one day he realized that he was physically present yet emotionally absent from them. While sitting at the dinner table, he realized that mentally he had been out to lunch. While driving his son to a soccer game, he could feel that he was emotionally detached, just as his father had been. For Matthew, yesterday's hurt had produced fresh fear and new rage. Even worst, it quenched the intimacy that he longed for.

Aunt Agony says the past can act like a monster squid from 20,000 leagues under the sea. "Of course most of you are not old enough to remember Kirk Douglass and Nemo. Nemo is the captain of the ship, not a fish in the movie, hun. It is best to cut up the sea monster of the past and create something new—calamari!" she said laughing. "Deep fry those 'back in the day' tentacles so they can't squeeze the future out of your marriage."

Oftentimes, to prove ourselves, our past shapes our self-esteem and convinces us that we have to play games. Life experiences warp and change us and we begin to judge every man or potential male friend by the one who wronged us. We are tempted to believe that every man has the potential to treat us like a Jacob and every woman has the potential to treat us like Rachel.

At an early age, Leah and Adrienne learned the meaning of victimization. Leah's light didn't shine as bright as Rachel's. Perhaps, she learned this while growing up and it continued into her marriage.

There are many Leahs in the world. Almost every woman owns a piece of Leah's story. Perhaps her story has not played out in your life the way it has played out in Leah's life. Almost everyone, however, has experienced sibling rivalry, betrayal by a family member, being unloved or unwanted, wanting who you can't have, or being viewed as a commodity to be loved and abruptly left.

Adrienne and Ariel were playing games with each other's lives. Game playing exacts a high price when it impacts the lives of others. Rachel and Leah were playing the game of chess. One would say "check" and the other "checkmate." They added new spouses and children whenever needed.

And again, we hurt those closest to us. "Father, forgive us for we know not what we do."

Jacob didn't take the time to assure Rachel or Leah that he valued them and God beyond what their wombs produced. He failed to manage the conflicts within his tents, he failed to soothe the pain, and he failed to reduce fear among each sister and their servants. He ignored their rumblings and left them to solve their sibling rivalry and competition. He was a part of the problem, not the solution to the problem.

Maleeta and her sister Trudella are best friends. Regretfully, this was not always the case. They went through a period of conflict and confrontation about everything, including men, personal wardrobe choices, and finances. As grown women, they chose to live on opposite sides of town, each seeing the other only at mandatory holiday family events.

One day, their mother became ill. The sisters returned home to provide care and support because their father was physically unable to help. Mal and Tru rekindled a strained relationship at her bedside.

Mal was tired of trying to keep things together for home and husband, career, and children. Tru loved her husband but he didn't do very well with discussions about mammograms and visits to the OB-GYN.

Over a cup of green tea latte, they realized that they had almost missed an opportunity to create a safe place where they could shake their dreg locks in that space between getting home and getting dinner ready. They realized that they had lost the gift of friendship that sisterhood, whether by blood or circumstance, means in a woman's life.

Ariel and Adrienne were not able to stop scalping and stabbing each other. The twins were out of control. They didn't realize that there were no winners in the game they were playing.

Mal and Tru were able to smooth the rough edges of their sibling rivalry and regain a fresh friendship. All close relationships have the potential to give us the greatest joy or the greatest sorrow. They can either provide a soft landing when we need it or a swift kick in the ego.

There is obvious sexual tension among Rachel, Jacob, and Leah, as well as the two other servants who became intimately involved with Jacob. As one of the members from our married couple's ministry said, it appeared that the act of sex had been transformed from a pleasurable experience to an experience where each women felt loneliness and powerlessness. It exposed jealousy and sibling rivalry among the participants. It made the vulnerable subservient and weak. Those who had the upper hand had a strong sense of control.

Reuben went to the fields during the wheat harvest. He found mandrake plants and was bringing them home to his mother Leah. The mandrake's fleshly forked roots resembled the lower part of the human body. Those who were superstitious believed that, when eaten, the plants could cause a woman to get pregnant.

Rachel asked Leah to give her the mandrakes. Her request was met with a hostile response: "It should have been enough that you took my husband but you'd take my son's good fortune as well?"

Rachel acquiesced. She traded her husband's sexual favors for Leah's mandrakes. Jacob would spend the night in Leah's tent, not her sister's.

One evening, as Jacob approached home after a long day in the fields, Leah approached him with her news: "You must sleep with me," she said. "I have hired you with my son's mandrakes." Silent Jacob spends the night with Leah like a prostitute hired for the night.

Whether it was the mandrakes or Leah's fertility, she conceives and Issachar is born. This was followed by the birth of Zebulum and later a daughter, Dinah.

God remembered Rachel and opened her womb. She became pregnant and said, "God has taken away my disgrace." She named her son Joseph and said, "May the Lord add to me another son." (Genesis 30:19–24) After Joseph was born, Jacob made plans to return home.

When I asked couples what they liked about being married, the responses are always varied. One person said she likes that she had someone with whom to share "the good, the bad and the ugly." Others said it was great to have someone to love and be loved in return, someone to share their lives with, someone to talk to, and, of course, someone to have a committed sexual relationship with.

What the world looks like to us determines the way we interpret it. If we see the world as a game to be played, we treat people like pieces on a chess board to be moved at our pleasure. If we see the world as hostile, everything and everyone is interpreted as an enemy. If we see the world as an opportunity, we will take advantage of its offerings.

If we see the world as safe, we enter it with confidence. If we feel the world owes us something, then we enter it looking for an entitlement. If we feel that the world is abusive, we do not trust it. If we feel that the world is full of strangers, we enter it disconnected. If we see the world as sacred space and life as precious, we will treat it with respect.

Rachel saw her life as a game that she must win. What did she really win? She won a life that was in constant turmoil. She won a home where the climate was filled with strife and arguments. She won a home where every thought, act, and movement was consumed with winning over your enemy—even though the enemy was her sister.

There is an enemy of our faith in Jesus Christ who will pit sister against sister, sibling against sibling and husband against wife. When we realize that we haven't changed old behavior patterns but have perpetuated them in our relationships, we can begin the process of healing and move towards reconciliation.

Aunt Agony says it is not too late to become friends with your spouse's brother or sister. "Cease fire!" she said. "No one wins except the lawyers who are happy to take your money."

"Plans fail for lack of counsel, but with many advisers, they will succeed." (Proverbs 15:22) Seek wise counsel from Godly mature persons such as a pastor, a pastoral counselor, a Christian marriage counselor, or a couple whose marriage has lasted more than a decade.

"Stop calling each other names is a good place to start," says Aunt Agony. "You are not a child anymore and neither is he. It's time for an upgrade."

Initiate reconciliation without being inflexible or willful. Own up to your part in the rivalry equation and resist those who try to suck you back into competition with a spouse or sibling. Make every effort to attend family functions. If you can't stay the whole time, at least make an appearance. It takes time to repair a relationship. It takes time to build one.

Learn how to be there for each other during the rough times. Celebrate his success whether or not he celebrates yours. Set the example by understanding your own value and worth to God and others.

Being envious of your sibling or spouse because you *think* they have an advantage or they have more than you is a waste of your time. Stop comparing notes, children, jobs, salaries, houses, cars, community service and/or service in the church.

There are two more important things to know. First, identify a shared interest with each sibling or with your spouse. This will enable you to identify your common ground and allow you to take advantage of its location. Second, forgive.

In his role as a historian, the physician Luke, who was Paul's companion, kept careful records of the early church. He wrote a careful chronological summary of events. Mark and John do not include the genesis of Jesus. Luke, however, painted the humanity of Jesus by presenting him as the Son of Humankind who sought us and offered us eternal life.

Luke gives us a universal Jesus who sought a diverse audience, including the tax collector Zacheus, rich people like Lazarus, women like Mary and Martha, sick folk like the ten lepers, a bent over woman, and a man beside the pool of Bethesda.

Luke gives us a Jesus who uses simple stories to explain complicated theological concepts. We have a Messiah who is concerned about the lost. He makes his point by using a lost coin, a lost sheep, and two lost sons.

Luke presents us with a Christ who prays everywhere. It seems like he prayed all the time. Jesus prayed when he felt like it and when he didn't feel like it. Before he divided the boy's fish sandwich, he prayed. Before Lazarus' tomb, he prayed. He left his Disciples to pray. Jesus taught his disciples to pray when they asked him, "Lord, teach us to pray."

At the Passover meal, where he instituted a new covenant based on his broken body and shed blood, he prayed. He prayed on the Mount of Temptation, on the Mount of Transfiguration, in the Garden of Gethsemane, on the Mount of Olives, and on Calvary's hill. And more important, while on the cross, Jesus prayed.

Forgiveness is a good place to start the journey towards reconciliation with your spouse or siblings. Forgiveness is predicated upon something that has been wrongly done to another. Humanity has a track record of inhumanity toward others, indicating that we are not kind to each other. This unkindness is called sin.

In spite of this, as humans we enjoy being in community. We are social beings. There are times when we can't get along with those who might have hurt us but we can't live without them. We do not flourish well in isolation.

Isolation is different from being alone. Living alone is the absence of people in your living space, not the absence of people from your life. Isolation is a cutoff notice from the world.

The significance of these two realities is that we either learn to forgive one another or engage in self-destructive actions. The self-inflicting responses include things like revenge, bitterness, hatred, being stuck on what's wrong or what went wrong. These are the things that will keep you up at night while others sleep peacefully.

"Reconcile or perish," cries Aunt Agony.

The core element of reconciliation between sinners is forgiveness. Remember, we are all sinners who have fallen short of God's glory. We can learn to forgive or we can whither away.

There are those who think that by withholding their forgiveness, the transgressor is being punished. The burden is borne by the one who forgives, not the one to be forgiven.

Forgiving someone doesn't mean that you tolerate someone's behavior or that you allow the person to hurt you again—as if nothing had happened. It means you have decided to free your spirit and let it go.

The fabric of the relationship is ripped open by the transgression. It closes a door in the other person's heart. We may have a hard time keeping the door open but we should resist locking the door.

We are tempted to lock the door, to remove the door, or to build a wall around it. When we withhold forgiveness, we lock the door to our heart. By keeping the door unlocked, we give our spouse, brother, and/or sister the chance to restore the relationship at anytime. They are waiting to receive permission from you to knock on the door. And they are waiting for you to say, "Come in."

Luke records that on the day of Jesus' crucifixion, Jesus does not pray for the good and the innocent. He prayed, "Father forgive them. . . ."

(Luke 23:32–34) Jesus prayed for people who had committed horrendous acts. He prayed for those who had enacted sadistic acts and offered them to God's mercy. It is for his enemies that he prayed saying, "Father, forgive them. . . ."

Jesus prays with the suggestion that those who have sinned do not fully understand what they have done. They do not comprehend the evil that has taken up residence in their hearts. He, however, still prayed for them without betraying his teachings on prayer—"pray for your enemies and those who spitefully use you and forgive them seventy times seventy."

Forgiveness will not change the past but it has the power to change the future. Forgiveness doesn't change the past; it expands the future.

God's forgiveness defies human understanding. We see that no one is beyond God's reach. There is nothing you can say or do to put you beyond the reach of Jesus' prayers. It also means that spouses and siblings are not beyond that reach.

Jesus prays a prayer of forgiveness for those who least deserved it. It cannot be earned or purchased from the throne of a cross. Hear them again as if you are hearing it for the first time—you forgive and it secures your forgiveness. Pray for those who have acted as enemies towards you and let them go.

According to published reports, in March, 1981, Beulah Mae McDonald dreamed she had a steel gray casket in her living room. When she woke up, she went to the room of her youngest son, Michael. Michael was not there. When the morning dawned, he still had not come home.

Her phone suddenly rang. She was told that there had been a party on the previous evening and that her son had been killed. She needed to come right away. Isolation becomes an attractive entity when the mess of rivalry and competition between siblings and spouses confronts you.

McDonald lived in a diverse neighborhood close to the Mobile, Alabama, police station. She was told that her son's body was found hanging from a tree. Across the street from her home lived the 64-year-old titan of the United Klans of America. It was reported that he said the hanging would look good on the news. And, further, that the hanging would look good for the Klan.

Michael's killers thought they would get away with the crime. They did. And because of this, Beulah Mae McDonald filed a civil lawsuit seeking damages totaling $7 million. She won. In the crowded court-room, the tears flowed. One of the murderers told Mrs. McDonald, "I cannot bring your son back, but if I could, I would trade places."

Beulah Mae McDonald then spoke. It is said that she forgave her son's murderers. Further, she told them that from the day she had found out who had killed her son, she had asked God to take care of them. And God had answered her prayers—"Father forgive them for they know not what they do."

Our understanding of reciprocity is enlarged. It is expanded from a limited group of people—family and friends or loved ones—to those whom we do not expect anything in return, our enemies.

Luke defines forgiveness as the ability to release, to liberate, and to let go. Jesus said let it go, not because he had to but because he wanted to.

Archibald Hart said forgive. It means relinquishing your right to hurt someone. God, please forgive them for refusing to destroy the bridge of the past. Let it go!

God released you. Now you need to release those who have hurt you. Forgive us our debts as we forgive those who trespass against us—even our enemies.

It was terrible for Ariel and Adrienne. Let it go! It was messy for Cassie. Let it go! It was a sadistic act. Let it go! It was abusive for Matthew. Let it go! It was horrendous for Rachel. Let it go! They wronged Leah. Let it go! It was premeditated. Let it go! It was wretched. Let it go! It was shameful. Let it go! They did it more than once. Let it go! They lied. Let it go! They talked about you. Let it go. They did it on purpose. Let it go! They killed your dreams. Let it go! They murdered your plans. Let it go! They broke your heart. Let it go! They died on you. Let it go! They spread rumors about you. Let it go! They impregnated you. Let it go! They stole your stuff. Let it go! They fired you. Let it go! They took you to court. Let it go! They high jacked your stuff. Let it go!

Let the voice of Jesus speak to your heart: "Father forgive them for they know not what they do." Now, let it go. Jesus prayed the prayer of forgiveness for things that were hard for us to let go. He couldn't leave until he had let it go.

After years of rivalry and competition, we need to be empowered to reconcile with a spouse or sibling. The author of Romans encourages the believer to begin a new life in Jesus Christ. Faith in Jesus Christ brings liberty and righteousness. Rather than being led by our own volition, we can be a part of those who are led by the Spirit. (Romans 8:12–17)

The Holy Spirit is mentioned nineteen times in the book of Romans. It is here where we learn that the Holy Spirit is given to the believer so that a new life can begin. The Holy Spirit helps us break through the walls of guilt and sin. The Holy Spirit frees us from a life of fear, dissatisfaction, and disappointment. Jesus is the focus of the relationship, not material things.

The Holy Spirit elevates us above basic human nature. Thus, we are led by the Spirit to be above the whims and will of society and culture. The Holy Spirit elevates our vision by moving our eyes from self to Christ. It lifts our view from earthly things to the spiritual nature of God that is eternal.

Before anyone else, God knew our potential and believed in us. God can see the road ahead of us and knows that what is required is beyond human capability. The Holy Spirit was given to us so that we might have the Fruit of the Spirit to conform to the character of Christ. Further, we have the Gift of the Spirit to empower us. This power brings out our potential so that it will not be lost in day to day living and will edify the body of Christ.

Being led by the Spirit means many things. It means letting go and releasing your life into God's hands. Our lives are not a "Home Depot" where you can fix everything yourself. It means stepping back and allowing the Holy Spirit to lead you towards the future that God has planned for you. It is allowing the Holy Spirit to lead you in your relationships with spouse, siblings, children, friends, and other family members.

The Iditarod is a winter dog sled race that covers over 1,150 miles from Anchorage to Nome, Alaska. A story is told about a novice racer who gave his dogs the command to go. The race was difficult and long. He finished last.

The novice racer asked an experienced racer to critique his efforts. The veteran told him, "The dogs know where to go. You kept trying to tell the dogs where to go and you kept your foot on the brake."

The Holy Spirit knows the way. We may limit our success by putting on spiritual breaks and not relinquishing control to the Holy Spirit. Trust God with the results of the future and let go!

Being led by the Spirit also means that you make yourself available to be used by God. Peter was available and preached his trial sermon on the day of Pentecost and 3,000 souls were saved. Paul and Silas were available to have midnight prayer meetings in jail. The jailer and his whole family were saved. Barnabus was available and gave lessons in encouragement. Stephen was available and received a standing ovation in heaven.

Be available to the Holy Spirit. Every day, live your life in such a way that the Spirit can lead you. When you make yourself available to the Spirit, your days will never be boring and always an adventure. With the supernatural empowerment of the Spirit, God gives us power to rise above the ordinary. Allow the Holy Spirit to lead you through reconciliation with your spouse, sibling, and others.

S.M.A.R.T. MOVES
(Spiritual Motivation for Action and Real Transformation)

Talking Points

1. Does rivalry interfere with you being a spouse, family member, or co-worker?
2. Do you compare yourself to your spouse or sibling(s)?
3. Is there anything in the past that reaches to strangle the life out of your future?
4. Were you favored by a parent and/or do you have a favorite child?
5. Are negative things from your past relationships repeating in your current relationships?
6. Do you or do you know anyone who seems to seek "a replacement parent" instead of a spouse?
7. In what ways would you defuse sibling rivalry or competition between you and your spouse?
8. In your heart, have you forgiven your spouse or family member for past hurts?

The Word of God

"As a bridegroom rejoices over his brides, so will you my God, rejoice over me. (Isaiah 62:5)

"I ask you to forgive your brothers the sins and the wrongs they committed in treating you so badly. . . ." (Genesis 50:17)

"Forgive us our sins, for we also forgive everyone who sins against us." (Luke 11:4)

The Word of Prayer

Create in me a clean heart, O God, and renew a new spirit and right spirit within me. I offer my body as a living sacrifice, holy and pleasing to you. Help my soul find rest in you. You are my rock, my salvation, my sword, and my shield. You are my fortress and I shall not be shaken by favoritism, unrealistic expectations, rivalry and competition with my family. At all times, help me to trust in you. For you and you alone are my refuge. In Jesus' name, Amen.

Foreplay

Before jumping out of the bed to begin your day, spend a few moments just holding hands with your spouse. Demonstrate affection in one small way before leaving the house—fix him a cup of tea or coffee—turn on the shower water, run the bath, get the kids ready for school or say words of admiration, make breakfast, or just snuggle up in bed together.

Pillow Talk

Do not compete with your spouse with language that implies "My day was better than your day" or "My day was worse than your day."

Kiss and Tell

Kiss or hug your spouse and members of your family. Tell them that you will be thinking good thoughts about them today. And do it for real!

Kiss and Make up

Today, forgive a family member or spouse who has caused pain or conflict. If you need to be forgiven, say, "I'm sorry."

Marital Madness

"Crazy making" is a covert form of competition where you crave the attention and affection of your children and spouse. It is also playing favorites with your children.

Singularity

Pray and ask God for guidance. Then send a "thinking of you" note to a rival sibling or family member. It is a step towards reconciliation.

EPILOGUE

Jacob also went on his way,
and the angels of God met him.

Genesis 32:1

Loving is lak de sea. It is a 'moving' thing,
but still and all, it takes its shape from de shore it
meets and it's different with every shore.

Zora Neale Hurston

Their Eyes Were Watching God

I t is amazing that God was able to work in and through the tangled relationships of Jacob and Rachel and Leah. It was a struggle to produce
a nation through Jacob, a person who was not always the best example.
Jacob, the deceiver had become Jacob, the favored of God. Conditions
were not perfect. Things were not right. People were not infallible yet
God chose Jacob to be the standard bearer in the founding of Israel.

Jacob's misfortune began when he misused Isaac, the God of his father, without having his own personal relationship with Isaac. A flight to
escape being murdered by his brother became a journey of maturation.
He left home with nothing and returned wiser and wealthier, bearing
wives, children and a herd of cattle.

In the end, when Jacob finally reconciled with his brother Esau, he had his own testimony. Jacob was now able to testify about the God who had sustained him for twenty years while he lived with his Uncle Laban. The challenges of a polygamous familial relationship had certainly tested his faith.

God was able to initiate Israel not because of Jacob's weaknesses but because of his strengths. A part of his strengths was his ability to learn and adapt to change. In spite of his deceitful and manipulative ways, he had a teachable spirit. This was unlike his brother Esau, who made hasty, thoughtless decisions such as exchanging his birthright for a bowl of soup.

Jacob wasn't perfect and neither are you or me. It is not that God overlooked Jacob's imperfections. God was able to maneuver around the imperfections to achieve the covenant promise. Jacob suffered the consequences of his actions and he had to live with the decisions he made.

Jacob, however, found favor with God.

A preacher friend of mine often says that "favor ain't fair!" God's favor changes the status quo. The expected and the usual are interrupted. Right under the noses of those who thought they had power and authority, the equation of power and authority was reconfigured so that power was transferred to God's favored.

Esau thought he was favored by God but the blessing and birthright belonged to Jacob. Rachel thought she had God's favor but Jacob's first born was borne by Leah. Joseph's brothers thought they had God's favor but power and authority was transferred from the eldest to the youngest, Joseph. Potiphar thought he had God's favor but the enslaved Joseph became the captain of his ruler's business. The jailer thought he had God's favor but the captured Joseph was catapulted from prisoner to second in command behind Pharaoh.

Mary found favor with God. She was an adolescent with no outstanding achievements but she was elevated to be the holy mother of God's son. Esther found favor with God. She was an orphan among her captors but became the queen who saved her people from genocide.

Jacob learned that God had the power to bless him in difficult places. Favor is when God allows the plum tree to blossom in early spring. It is one of the first flowering trees in many places in North America. It blooms at a dangerous and difficult time when frost, ice and snow can shorten its life. Nevertheless, it blooms in spite of the winter cold.

This is how the favor of God works. You may want to bloom but it may be too early for you to bloom because there are too many risks. You might live in a poor location. You might have a poor track record. You might also have a plethora of weaknesses yet because of God's favor, what looked like a disaster can become an opportunity to succeed.

The difficult reality of relationships similar to Jacob, Rachel and Leah is that the church does not want to acknowledge the struggles of married couples and those seeking covenant relationships. Gilbert H. Caldwell writes that the pulpit should be the locus for preaching and teaching. Therefore, the church should be the place for "sexual healing.".

If we are going to serve the present age, we cannot continue to deny the reality of what goes on inside and outside of the household of faith. The stories in *Swapping Housewives* are real. Christians struggle with issues such as homosexuality, pornography, gambling, incarceration, thug-life, sibling rivalry, jealousy, envy, and dishonesty.

There is another message of encouragement that I need to share. God can gift you to be a blessing to your spouse and/or children. "Forever love" is an invitation to open one's life to another. A Circle of Love sister said that after all her years of pretending to be grown; it was her marriage that taught her how to be an adult!

Marriage can challenge you and even infuriate you as you learn how to live with someone who may want to do things differently.

Marriage is a shared adventure with peaks and valleys.

"The reality of marriage is that sometimes it's fun and sometimes it's not," said another Circle member. "There are days when it is easy and days when it is hard."

"Truthfully, sometimes I don't like him. In fact, when my last nerve is plucked, I hate him. Sometimes, in the middle of the night, I look over at this person and wonder what am I doing here? Then he turns over, looks at me with those big brown eyes and smiles. Bang, I stop wondering why and go to sleep in the arms of the man who loves me!"

Delia said she wasn't prepared to handle the good times and bad times with someone else. She was use to dealing with things on her own. She was willing to share her home but not her life.

You learn how to care for another person's emotional needs in a marriage. Marsha said she learned that she needed daily affection and each day, her husband needed to be affirmed. He learned that she needed to be touched, held and kissed. She learned that his need for touching, holding and kissing, led to other desires. He learned that she needed to talk. She learned that he needed quiet time. He learned how to make her laugh and she learned that she could make him cry.

Marriage is work. Marriage is learning how to balance life. There must be balance between togetherness and separateness, grace and mercy, work and play, and routine and recreation.

Aunt Agony would remind you that "ordinary doesn't have to be boring and repetition doesn't make it right!"

Marriage can be great and still be a breeding ground for discontent.

"When I got married, I thought my husband would meet all of my needs. I was mistaken. God is the supplier of all my needs, not the man I live with," she said.

Samuel Johnson writes that great works are not performed by strength but by perseverance. Another writer concluded that nothing good is achieved without a struggle. Still, yet another writer shared that one's talents and abilities are not enough. One must have the ability to struggle on a course without distraction or diversion.

"If you're lazy on the job, you'll get fired," says Aunt Agony. "If you're lazy about your marriage, sweetie, it's the same thing!"

It is amazing how God worked through the convoluted relationships of Jacob and Rachel and Leah. Further, God's amazing love continues to be the artesian springs from which we draw resources for our own relationships.

Love well, my brothers and sisters. Love forever!

"Love as long as you can," says Aunt Agony. "When you can't love anymore then restart your engine!"

BIBLIOGRAPHY

Barash, Susan Shapiro. *Tripping the Prom Queen: The Truth about Women and Rivalry.* New York: St Martin's Press, 2006.

Burton, Valorie. *What's Holding You Back? Closing the Gap Between Where You Are and Where You Want to Be.* Colorado Springs: Waterbrook Press, 2005.

Bynum, Juanita. *Matters of the Heart.* Lake Mary: Charisma House, 2002.

Eggerichs, Emerson. *Love & Respect: The Love She Most Desires, the Respect He Desperately Needs.* Nashville: Integrity, 2004.

Eldredge, John, and Stasi Eldredge. *Captivating: Unveiling the Mystery of a Woman's Soul.* Nashville: Nelson Books, 2005.

Eldredge, John. *The Journey of Desire: The Participant's Guide.* Nashville: Thomas Nelson. 2000

Ethridge, Shannon, and Greg Ethridge. *Every Woman's Marriage: Igniting the Joy and Passion You Both Desire.* Colorado Springs: Waterbrook P, 2006.

Friel, John C., and Linda D. Friel. *The 7 Best Things (Happy) Couples Do.* Deerfield Beach: Health Communications, 2002.

Harrar, Sari, and Rita Demaria. *The 7 Stages of Marriage: Laughter, Intimacy, and Passion: Today, Tomorrow, and Forever.* Pleasantville: Reader's Digest Association, 2006.

Hendrix, Harville, and Helen L. Hunt. *Getting the Love You Want Workbook.* New York: Atria Books, 2003.

Hendrix, Harville. *Getting the Love You Want: A Guide for Couples.* New York: Henry Holt, 2001.

Kirshenbaum, Richard, and Daniel Rosenberg. *Closing the Deal: Two Married Guys Reveal the Dirty Truth to Getting Your Man to Commit.* New York: W. Morrow, 2005.

Lamm, Maurice. *The Power of Hope: The One Essential of Life and Love.* New York: Rawson Associates, 1995.

McGee, Robert S. *The Search for Significance.* Nashville: W Group, 2003.

McKinney-Hammond, Michelle. *What to Do Until Love Finds You.* Eugene: Harvest House, 1997.

McLaughlin, Mignon. *The Complete Neurotic's Notebook.* Edinburgh: Castle Books, 1981.

McManus, Erwin. *Chasing Daylight: Seize the Power of Every Moment.* Nashville: Thomas Nelson, 2006.

Miracle, T., Miracle A., Baumeister. *Human Sexuality: Meeting Your Basic Needs.* Academic Internet Publisher, 2006.

Moore, Beth. *Get Out of That Pit.* Nashville: Integrity, 2007.

Omartian, Stormie. *The Power of a Praying Wife.* Eugene: Harvest House Publishers, 2007.

Parrott, Les, and Leslie Parrott. *'Saving Your Marriage Before It Starts: Seven Questions to Ask Before and After You Marry.* Grand Rapids: Zondervan, 2006.

Pipher, Mary. *The Shelter of Each Other: Rebuilding Our Families* New York: Ballantine Books, 1997.

Potter-Efron, Ronald T., and Patricia S. Potter-Efron. *Reclaim You Relationship: A Workbook of Exercises and Techniques to Help You Reconnect with Your Partner.* Hoboken: Wiley, 2006.

Real, Terrence. *The New Rules of Marriage: What You Need to Know to Make Love Work.* New York: Ballantine Books, 2007.

Robertson, Annabelle. *The Southern Girl's Guide to Surviving the Newlywed Years.* New York: New American Library, 2007.

Schlessinger, Laura. *Ten Stupid Things Men Do to Mess Up their Lives.* New York: HarperPerennial, 1998.

Seligman, Martin E. *Learned Optimism: How to Change Your Mind and Your Life.* New York: Simon & Shuster, 1998

Smalley, Gary. *Making Love Last Forever.* Dallas: Word Group, 1996.

Smith, Robin L. *Lies At the Altar: The Truth About Great Marriages.* New York: Hyperion, 2006.

Steinberg, Robert. *The Triangle of Love: Intimacy, Compassion, Commitment.* New York: Basic Books, 1988

Washington, Denzel, comp. *A Hand to Guide Me.* Des Moines: Meredith Books, 2006.

Yudkowsky, Moshe. *The Pebble and the Avalanche: How Taking Things Apart Creates Revolutions.* San Francisco: Berrett-Koehler Publishers, 2005.